Do I Love God?

Do I Love God?

The Question That Must Be Answered

R OD C ULBERTSON

WIPF & STOCK · Eugene, Oregon

Wipf & Stock
An Imprint of Wipf and Stock Publishers
199 W. 8th Ave., Suite 3
Eugene, OR 97401

www.wipfandstock.com

PAPERBACK ISBN: 978-1-5326-1920-5
HARDCOVER ISBN: 978-1-4982-4540-1
EBOOK ISBN: 978-1-4982-4539-5

Manufactured in the U.S.A.   AUGUST 21, 2017

With the deep assurance that my love for God, although much more smoke than fire, is due solely to the work of the Holy Spirit in my life, I dedicate this book to the third person of the Trinity. Like the Father and the Son, he is eternally full of love and life and is most certainly the one who has sovereignly and lovingly sheltered me from harm, gently wooed me, convicted me of sin, drawn me with his power, graciously changed my heart, and transformed me, while continuing to remain faithfully involved in my life on a daily basis. Despite my constant self-will, obstinacy, self-reliance, and self-serving nature, he has placed a love in my heart for both God and others, a love that I could not generate in my own power. I am grateful to him for his work in my life. I worship the Holy Spirit, as the one who constantly assures me of both the love of the Father and the Son and testifies of the glory of the Lord Jesus. God's Spirit is the teacher who guides God's people as they learn how to love God with their minds, emotions, and wills. May he be praised and thanked!

Contents

Acknowledgments

B ooks are powerful influences, and in the formative years of my early Christian life reading was powerfully used by God to change my heart. I therefore express my deepest appreciation to the following authors who have stirred my mind, emotions, and will toward fully loving God: Dr. J. I. Packer, author of *Knowing God*; the late Rev. Mr. A. W. Tozer, author of *The Pursuit of God* and *The Knowledge of the Holy*; and the late Francis Schaeffer, author of *Two Contents: Two Realities*, among other publications.

In addition to these authors, I also wish to acknowledge the late Rev. Mr. Buck Hatch, longtime professor at Columbia International University, who taught me that my love for God is a response to his love for me. I can still hear Buck Hatch's voice, reassuring me of this truth.

A special word of thanks must be given to my RTS Charlotte teaching assistant, Ms. Anna Unkefer, who spent countless hours editing this work and refining it for publication. She is an invaluable asset in my efforts toward publishing a book. Also, I must thank two other readers of this work who most certainly helped to improve it with their observations: Mrs. Tari Williamson, faithful servant of all; and RTS student Mrs. Karen Chacko, who encouraged me in the work. All of these ladies' assistance is deeply appreciated by the author.

Introduction

When my involvement in religion went from duty to delight,
I knew I was converted.

GEORGE WHITEFIELD

Enoch walked with God, and he was not, for God took him.

GENESIS 5:24

T he scene from my childhood is vividly etched in my memory—
I was around four or five years old and had crossed the street
in our very modest neighborhood over to the neighbor's yard that
was located catty-corner from our house. I was only fifty yards
from our front door! But, as I escaped from my own home, not
going too far, I found myself pursuing the experience that I still
love today—being by myself and alone with my thoughts. It was
a sunny, summer day replete with a clear blue sky. The neighbor's
yard was long and seemingly wide to a small child like myself, and
filled with lush, thick green grass. Everything around me was quiet
and I decided, on this pleasant day, to lay down on the flat grassy
spot in the neighbor's yard and relax for a few minutes. All alone!

I recall lying still and looking up into the heavens. Staring at the endless blue sky, I thought to myself, "There must be a God. And I really want to know him."

Certainly, I had been taught about God, both at home by my mother and at my church in Sunday school. I had heard about him during Sunday worship services, as well as while attending summer Vacation Bible Schools. But this was not Sunday school—there was something that seemed innate, a part of my being, to believing that this big world was made by a great God. Honestly, I never enjoyed church—none of it, except for the friends and the sports teams. Growing up, fully immersed in the activities of a Southern Baptist church (and fully immersed at age six as well), I resented church and almost *all* of the church activities. I endured it because church was required and in spite of attending almost all of the services and meetings (I used to pray on Saturday nights in the winter time that it would snow, shutting down the city!), I didn't know God. At times, I hated him! When I prayed, I felt like my prayers stopped at the ceiling or went nowhere, or that God was so far away that I would never reach him. Could I know God? Did I really want to know him? He seemed to stand in the way of my happiness and I was certain that he was not the route to my personal fulfillment or the abundant life.

I reluctantly attended church throughout my high school years. I heard a lot about God and Jesus but nothing impacted me very much, except for some of the moral persuasions; and although my outward behavior was exemplary to many observers, my heart was dark and my life was filled with both selfishness and deep insecurity. I went off to college convinced that I could leave these plaguing God-concepts behind. I would run from God and forge out on my own at the big state school, the University of South Carolina! I not only didn't know God at this point, I had no interest in loving him at all. But running didn't work—you can't outrun God, and if he has his eye on you, you will not escape. Not escaping God's good hand is one aspect of what we call grace.

Grace is God's choosing to call you to himself even when you don't want him in your life. He saves you from self-destruction (which is the consequence of the self-driven life) and from self-salvation (which never works because of our sins and failures—God requires perfection). Grace is God showering his love and compassion upon people who are rebels in thought, word, and deed, and drawing them to personally find him at the foot of the cross. Without going into details, as my life seemed to be falling apart during my freshman year in college, God grabbed my attention and showed me his grace. I turned my life over to him and understood that trusting in Christ for salvation meant that I was committed to giving everything over to God—there would be no looking back. Becoming a true Christian (many would have said I already was a Christian, though it didn't seem so) involved some trauma to the self-life and I was shaken up to a good extent. But the joy, love, peace, and life transformation that I experienced was unlike anything I had ever known before. In my heart, I knew that "I now know God," the God I had wanted and wished for back in my early childhood days. The experience was soulfully exhilarating and brought more freedom and liberation to my life than I could ever imagine. I realized that I could know God and not only could I know him—my creator—personally, I now could pursue this relationship in such a way that I could love God with my whole being.

PURPOSE OF THE BOOK

The purpose of this book is to help us answer the question, "Do I love God?" I am writing on the basis (or the assumption) that God exists, that we can pursue him by faith, and that he is a rewarder of those who diligently seek him (Hebrews 11:6). The God of the Bible is both living and a Trinity—Father, Son, and Holy Spirit. God is one, but he exists in and reveals himself in three persons. Love exists only because God has existed eternally, pouring out his love continuously for all time, the Father toward the Son and the Spirit, the Son toward the Father and the Spirit, and the Holy Spirit toward the Father and the Son. Who can comprehend it?—this three-person loving relationship existing from eternity—but it defines the one, true God. Because God is both triune (a trinity of persons, loving one another in full and perfect relationship from eternity) and relational, we, who are made in his image, can actually know him personally and walk in loving relationship with him. God is not impersonal; he is love. Loving God is why we are created. Only our sins and the self-life can prevent us from knowing and loving God.

So, the question for each of us is, "Do I love God?" I might ask, "Do *you* love God?" but the reality is that I always must pose this question to myself as well. As a matter of fact, it is a question that I feel obligated to ask myself constantly, since Jesus himself declared, "You shall love the Lord your God with all your heart and with all your soul and with all your mind" (Matthew 22:37). Why do I exist? To know, love, and glorify the living God, maker of the universe! I hope that together we can understand more fully what it means to love our glorious God.

Do I Love God?

As we attempt to answer *the* question, "Do I love God?" I would like to begin by asking a series of related questions simply for personal reflection.

1. Do you love *the things* of God? That is, when you think about God—his creation and his world, his church, his kingdom, his worth and worship, his greatness and work, etc.—is your heart touched and moved? When you consider the kingdom of God—its growth and your service in it—does your spirit soar? Does your heart rejoice? Are you truly interested in *the things* of God?

2. Do you love *the knowledge* of God? Do you love to study the Bible and Christian doctrines? Do you love learning, reading books, attending Sunday school or Bible classes, or studying as a teacher? Do you love listening to powerful or thought-provoking sermons? Are you amazed that *you* can have a Bible in your hands and read and study God's Word in your own language? Are you grateful for all of the books you can read that teach you about God?

3. Do you love *serving* God? Do you love doing ministry, explaining the gospel, helping the hurting, the struggling, the doubting, and the needy? Do you love teaching others and leading and being a part of small group ministries? Do you love discipling other believers and spending time with those questioning and willing to learn? Do you love acts of mercy on behalf of God? Do you delight in doing God's work?

Having asked those three questions, I return to the question of this book: "Do I love God?" (or, "Do you love God?") In some ways, this is a different question from the previous questions. They dealt with *things, knowledge,* and *service.* The question of the book is, "Do you have emotions and passion for, and devotion to, the one living and true God, as well as a settled commitment that he is the Lord of your life and everything to you?" Is Jesus really the pearl of great price in your life, the greatest possible possession you can imagine or that you could ever cherish?

Motivation

The first three questions above lead me to ask a further question: "How do you know (that you love God)?" If I asked you to explain your love to God, how would you do it? Better yet, the question might pinpoint a deeper issue: "What motivates you? What is your motivation in the Christian life?" I am fascinated with the topic of motivation. Why do people do what they do? The first research paper I wrote in college was entitled "Motivation of the Athlete." What prompts the athlete to strive for a superior performance or for final victory? Better yet, what prompts me to strive to know God and to cross the finish line well into eternity? Is our motivation linked to our passion for God, or are we motivated by something else? I have read that the late Dr. Jack Miller, pastor, professor, and author, would ask his Westminster Seminary students this question each semester: "When is the last time you did something *purely* out of *love for God?*" What an overwhelming concept! I must honestly say that I don't think I have ever done anything *purely* out of love for

God. It seems that Rod Culbertson always has ulterior motives—I can't seem to escape self-preservation or self-promotion! "When is the last time that I did something purely out of love for God?" Possibly never, but I would like to contend that I do love God. Where there is smoke, I hope that there is at least a small fire manifesting a genuine love for God. I ask all of these questions in order to help us search our hearts. I know that I constantly have to search my own heart and I'm sure that everyone has some heart searching to do in regard to their relationship with God.

The Final Judgment?

The question remains: "Do I love God?" The renowned Puritan pastor Richard Baxter once attempted to describe what he thought might be a crucial issue of accountability as individuals face the final judgment of God. In his imagination, he surmised, "The question will not be, 'How much have you known, or professed, or talked?' but, 'How much have you loved?' *and* 'Where was your heart?'"[1] I believe that Richard Baxter understood well that God looks at the heart (1 Samuel 16:7), and that the Bible tells us that Jesus calls us to inspect our hearts (Matthew 15:17–20; 5:27–28). So, we must conclude that our secret thoughts and our motives are a true indicator of whether we love God. I do hope that you love the things of God. I also hope that you love the knowledge and study of God. Further, I'm sure I would be very encouraged if I knew that you love the service of God. But it is possible, and often the reality, that a person can be busy studying God or serving God, while at the same time neither knowing nor loving God!

Honestly?

The goal of this book is to bring this sad possibility—studying and serving God, but not actually loving him—to light and to solve it. In essence, I can tell you that I spent most of the early years of my

1. Demarest, *Satisfy Your Soul*, 166.

life in a context in which it appeared that I was a Christian. I did *all* (or almost all) of the things that Christians were supposed to *do*! I learned all sorts of Christian, biblical, and Baptist doctrines. I was quick at doing sword drills (a game or activity in which individuals attempt to find a Bible verse first, i.e., prior to the others competing). I memorized numerous Bible verses as a child, taught a Bible lesson to my peers in the seventh grade (just try that once!), walked down the aisle two different times during altar calls, was baptized, and was inside the church building almost every time the doors were open. Only an extreme case of shyness prevented me from doing church follow-up visitation (door knocking), singing in the youth choir, going on camp-outs with the other youth, or leading the youth group in any way. Churched? Yes! Christian? I don't think so. What motivated me? Duty, guilt, legalism, adult disapproval (or approval), as well as fear of temporal (and probably eternal) judgment. As I mentioned earlier, I hated church and sometimes I hated God—the God who was in control of everything, especially my life. But I was present in body and Christian in appearance. If someone had asked me then, "Do you love God?" I probably would have lied and said "Yes." To some extent, I did want God, but in reality I loved myself first and foremost! It is easy to be deceived about whether or not you love God.

QUESTIONS FOR REFLECTION

1. How does the self-directed life prevent our love for God?

2. Why is it so easy to replace heartfelt devotion to God with the "things of God," the "study of God," or the "service of God"? What are some examples of how we replace God with other Christian or "spiritual" activities?

3. When is the last time that you did something purely out of love for God?

4. What are some unhealthy motivations for living the Christian life?

5. What do you think of Richard Baxter's portrayal of the question that God might ask us at the final judgment, "How much have you loved?" and/or "Where was your heart?"

6. How does the local church, whose goal is to help us love God more, sometimes take the place of actually loving God?

ACTION POINTS

1. Set aside twenty minutes to pray and reflect upon your own motivations for Christian service. Read through Philippians 3:1–17 and list the good and bad motivations that drove the Apostle Paul. Meditate on your own motivations and ask the Lord to refine anything that is false in your life.

2. Make a list of those things (good or bad) in your life that compete with seeking after God with your whole heart. Call them what they are—idols—and ask the Lord to help you to gain a proper perspective on how they fit into your life on a daily basis. Pray about your priorities as related to God.

PRAYER

"O Lord, I confess that I can so easily go through the motions of living out the Christian life, without pausing and taking serious time to contemplate who you are and to thus give you the praise and adoration you deserve. Help me to express wholehearted love to you. Remove from my heart those loves that prevent me from loving you fully. In Christ's holy name. Amen."

Chapter 1

Spirituality Reality Check

Every time we say we believe in the Holy Spirit,
we mean we believe that there is a living God able and
willing to enter human personality and change it.

JOHN OWEN

The Christian faith is ultimately not only a matter of doctrine
or understanding or of intellect, it is a condition of the heart.

DR. MARTYN LLOYD-JONES

TRUE SPIRITUALITY

As we continue to try to answer our question, "Do I love God?" and focus upon the heart of the matter, I am reminded of Pastor Richard Phillips's observation in his commentary on the book of Zechariah. Dr. Phillips asks the poignant question, "So, what is true religion? What does real spirituality look like?" He answers,

> First, it is a desire for God himself, for his pleasure and his glory; Second, it is concerned with the inner realities of sin and righteousness and only then with consequences and external blessings; Third, true spirituality is that which

draws from God's Word, hearing and believing and doing
according to what God has spoken in the Bible.[1]

The thoughtful Dr. Phillips fully understood that the person
who is truly spiritual desires God and his glory first and foremost.
The self is not exalted in, and self-centeredness is not a reflection
of, true spirituality. The person seeking true spirituality looks
within and discovers his need before God—sin is the inner problem and righteousness (or obedience) is the solution. Such obedience must be based on listening to God's Word, believing it, and
submitting to it. The doing must be driven by the motivations of
the heart, a heart for God that is in touch with its own sins, failures, and inadequacies, a heart so in touch with its sins that out of
its need springs a passion for God's righteousness and a reliance
upon God's strength.

THE HEART OF LEADERSHIP

In the leadership course that I teach at Reformed Theological Seminary, I tell the students that, among others (the list could be even
more extensive), there are twelve "Qualifications of Leadership"
necessary for effective ministry influence. Each consideration begins with the letter "C." These twelve considerations are:

1. Calling

2. Competence

3. Confidence

4. Character

5. Credibility

6. Conviction

7. Courage

8. Compatibility

9. Chemistry

1. Phillips, *Zechariah*, 159.

10. Commitment

11. Caring

12. Communication/Clarity

I remind our students, most of whom will go into a future ministry of some type, that although calling (the certainty that God's hand is on their lives) is the number one qualification for longevity in the ministry, the number one qualification for doing ministry is *character*! Character deals with *being*—it focuses upon the heart of the servant leader. I emphasize to them that character is who you are when no one else (or God alone) is looking. Character means that your heart, mind, and life belong to Christ, who is Lord over all that you do. Character ("Christlikeness," in Christian terms) is related to a heart that is dedicated to the Lord. Character is life lived *coram deo*, i.e., in the presence of or before the face of God! The deeper one's heart relationship with God becomes, the more reliable/developed their character becomes. The greatest source for character is a transformed heart, a heart fully devoted to God. Character may be demonstrated and observed by external behavior but true character is internal; it stems from a heart impacted by the gospel and submitted to the living Lord Jesus Christ.

A FEW THOUGHTS ABOUT LOVING GOD

In Dr. J. I. Packer's book *A Quest for Godliness*, he writes about the possible reality that believers can fall into a state of Christian "autopilotism," i.e., going through the motions, and consequently failing to have a heart experience of walking with God. He writes,

> When Christians meet, they talk to each other about their Christian work and Christian interests, their Christian acquaintances, the state of the churches, and the problems of theology—but rarely of *their daily experience of God* (emphasis mine). Modern Christian books and magazines contain much about Christian doctrine, Christian standards, problems of Christian conduct, techniques of Christian service—but little about the

inner realities of fellowship with God. Our sermons contain much sound doctrine, but little relating to the converse between the soul and the Savior. We do not spend much time, alone or together, in dwelling on the wonder of the fact that God and sinners have communion at all; no, we just take that for granted, and give our minds to other matters.[2]

In other words, believers often receive the gospel (or we might say "Christ into their lives"), find forgiveness, and then fall into a trap of Christian activity. They conclude, "I'm accepted by God, so everything's okay and I can just serve away . . ." The possibility that Christians can go through the motions, even doing so very well, exists even at times in the seminary environment. I have observed this reality at Reformed Theological Seminary. Upon graduation, at the end of the seminary journey, I have joyfully heard graduating students say, "I learned to trust God" or "My faith is stronger than when I came here" or "I love God more at the end of my seminary experience than when I began." Nevertheless, sadly, I have also heard them say when completing their seminary journey, "My walk with God was terrible while at seminary" or "My personal life with God stinks." Those that expressed such disappointment in their seminary training did admit that they were far too busy with studies or overloaded with either ministry or marriage and/ or family responsibilities. Their busyness led to the neglect of their personal spiritual life. What keeps you from loving God with a devoted, heartfelt love? Work, play, leisure, family, poor time management, technology, laziness, sin, or personal failure? The excuses and reasons are numerous and somehow allow us to ignore or underdevelop our relationship with God, the most important relationship in life. So, I conclude with one more question: "Are you growing in your love for God?"

2. Packer, *Quest for Godliness*, 215–16.

A STARK REALITY

Dr. Bruce Demarest has been a professor at Denver Seminary since 1975. He works closely with students in order to assist them in their spiritual growth. He explains some of the stark realities that he has seen and communicated during his many years of teaching and ministry. Here are a few of his observations.

- 48 percent of adults who regularly attend Christian churches have not experienced God's presence at any time in the last twelve months.

- According to George Barna, 36 percent of Evangelical Christians are still searching for meaning in life.

- "I've been a Christian and attended church for many years. But I have no idea what it means to have a relationship with Jesus. God is someone I pray to at night between the sheets when I'm in trouble." (church elder)

- Many believers remain infants in Christ (1 Cor 3:1), lacking vision, passion, and power.

- Only 52 percent of Christians are making some effort to grow spiritually. Many of these are inconsistent and get limited results.[3]

Pastor and author A. W. Tozer reiterates the tragic state of affairs that exists in the professing "Christian" community when he writes, "For millions of Christians, God is no more real than He is to non-Christians. They go through life trying to love an ideal and be loyal to a mere principle."[4] Tozer's statement is simply staggering, but I wonder if it might be a true appraisal of the average Christian in his day, as well as today. Tozer's quote begs us to ask the question, "Do I love God?" We are forced to confront ourselves and the church today with the question, "Are professing believers

---

3. Lecture notes from an RTS Charlotte 2007 Doctor of Ministry course, citing Barna, *Growing True Disciples*, 43.

4. Tozer, *Pursuit of God*, 50.

truly converted and saved?" Can the unconverted and those without a genuine relationship with God actually love him?

I still remember hearing two prominent evangelical leaders of the 1970s, Billy Graham and Bill Bright (Cru), both declare on more than one occasion, "90 to 95 percent of Christians do not have a victorious Christian life." In other words, both men were of the similar opinion that most Christians live defeated lives, absent of both victory over sin and the vibrant life of the indwelling Holy Spirit. We might argue that a completely defeated Christian is no Christian at all. But the reality is that many Christians do not grow in their faith because their lives and possibly their churches are devoid of the means of grace (or means of growth), particularly the preached Word of God. Professing Christians may go through the motions of looking like a Christian, but their lives and hearts may never have encountered the living God! As mentioned earlier, I still recall spending years of my youth sitting in worship services without actually worshipping or loving God. How can this be? Yet, I recall one of my more vivid memories in my early walk as a new Christian. It involved standing up while on the front row of the historic sanctuary of First Baptist Church of Columbia, South Carolina, on a fall Sunday morning. With the rest of the congregation, I was singing a hymn, and, for the first time ever, realized that I was not simply singing words—I was singing praise, from my heart, to the living God! It was a completely new experience and one for which I was grateful and at which I was amazed. Heartfelt religion is often missing from the practice of religious duties. Is this your experience? You must look inside your heart in order to answer the question, "Do I love God?"

IS GOD REAL TO ME?

Some years ago, due to my ministry with and to seminary students, I was asked to attend a conference sponsored by the Association of Theological Schools (ATS), the accrediting group for most of the major seminaries in the country, held in Tampa, Florida. I listened as the primary presenter, a former Roman Catholic priest (as I recall) explained the results of some of their (ATS) surveys of entering theological students across the broad spectrum of a number of diverse seminaries. As he went through some of the attributes of these students, for some reason he pointed out that three major denominations sent students (or potential/future ministry workers) into seminary training who had scored very low in a specific category. That category was "belief in God's providence," i.e., the belief that God is actively working in and through people in his world.

In other words, a substantial number of seminary students were pursuing a degree suited for future ministry, most likely in a local church or parish setting, but these same students did not appear to believe that God was vibrantly active and available as an intervening power on their behalf! I was the only conservative, Bible-believing Presbyterian representative in this small group of extremely diverse participants. I was amazed to hear this observation, but the lecturer's conclusions were not at all addressed by anyone else in the room. I could not fathom that this group of seminary employees were seemingly not alarmed at the instructor's observation. Could it be that the American church today is being led by people who don't even believe in a vital, daily, experiential relationship with the living God? I shudder at the thought, but do wonder if such a premise is true. Is there such a thing as Christianity without the life of Christ?

The nature of this pseudo-Christianity is further addressed by Dr. Demarest, as he explains the absence of spiritual reality in the lives of many people who profess faith. He contends that today's spirituality is deceptive in its appearance. He asks, "What does today's spirituality look like?" He answers, "Much religious activity with little transformation." He goes on to quote discipleship expert Dr. Bill Hull: "Even well-intentioned believers drift and find themselves nearly comatose spiritually, numbed by years of religious activity without transformation."[5] In a related thought, Anglican scholar and author Dr. J. I. Packer writes,

5. Hull, *Choose the Life*, 38.

. . . the experiential reality of perceiving God is unfamiliar territory today. The pace and preoccupations of urbanized, mechanized, collectivized, secularized modern life are such that any inner life (apart from the existential *Angst* of society's misfits and casualties of the rat race) is very hard to maintain. To make prayer your life priority, as countless Christians of former days did outside as well as inside the monastery, is stupendously difficult in a world that runs you off your feet and will not let you slow down. And if you attempt it, you will certainly seem eccentric to your peers, for nowadays involvement in a stream of programmed activities is "in" and the older idea of a quiet, contemplative life is just as decidedly "out" . . . the concept of a Christian life as sanctified rush and bustle still dominates and as a result the experiential side of Christian holiness remains very much a closed book.[6]

Dr. Demarest concludes, "The church has done a better job leading people to faith than nurturing their spiritual lives. The church is more effective in areas of knowing (knowledge) and doing than being." He reflects upon this situation, "Recovery of authentic Christian spirituality requires a turn to the heart— 'heart'—the core of the inner life; the integrating, control center of the person (Ps. 9:1; Mt. 18:35)."[7] What do you think—are believers in the church today demonstrating insipid faith? Is the heart of our faith being replaced by learning (the mind) and doing (the will)? Or are we simply paralyzed by indifference? And, more seriously, is the cause of the loss of heartfelt faith the fact that Christians have no vital, life-giving relationship with Christ and thus cannot clearly answer the question "Do I love God?"

---

6. Packer, *Keep in Step with the Spirit*, 64.

7. Lecture notes from RTS Charlotte course DM843, p. 15. Used with permission.

QUESTIONS FOR REFLECTION

1. If true spirituality is defined by dealing with the inner realities of sin and righteousness, why do we so easily default to defining true spirituality by our efforts or activities?

2. How does living life *coram deo*, i.e., in the presence of God, affect our character?

3. Whether or not "autopilotism" is an actual word, why is it that we often start going through the motions in the Christian life? How does going through the motions impact our relationship with God?

4. What do you personally think about the quote, "90 to 95 percent of Christians do not have a victorious Christian life"?

5. How does believing in God's providence impact our love for God? How would not believing in it affect us?

ACTION POINTS

1. If you do not already practice a habit or form of personal, daily devotions, find a quiet and private place and set aside fifteen minutes per day for the next week to read Scripture, pray, and meditate in God's presence. Read Matthew 5–7, commonly known as "The Sermon on the Mount," to help you with this spiritual discipline. Walk through the passage slowly and ask God to speak to your heart in a new way.

2. Before you rise out of bed in the morning this week, ask God to show himself to you in some real fashion and to work providentially in your life, in either a small or big way. Ask the Lord to help you experience the reality of his presence in a real way.

PRAYER

"O Lord, I believe; help my unbelief (Mark 9:24). I pray today that you will show me your glory and work in my life in such a way that I gain a greater assurance of your presence. And if you are quiet in my life, may I continue in loving trust of your faithfulness and power. I will seek you in your Word and I pray that in seeking I will find. Speak, O Lord; your servant is listening. Reveal your glory and demonstrate your power. Revive my soul by your Holy Spirit. In the name of your Son, Jesus, amen."

Chapter 2

What Is Most Important?

Without a doubt
the mightiest thought the mind can entertain is the thought of God.

A. W. TOZER

I have one desire now-to live a life of reckless abandon for the Lord,
putting all my energy and strength into it.

ELISABETH ELLIOT

IN WHAT DO YOU BOAST?

Almost forty years ago, at age twenty-two, I began searching for the future seminary that I would attend for my personal ministry training. In the initial stages of the search, in God's providence, while returning home by bus to South Carolina from a trip to Arrowhead Springs, California, I visited some friends who attended Southwestern Baptist Theological Seminary, located in Fort Worth, Texas. While spending a couple of days on the campus, I was invited by my host student, who was also a good friend of mine, to visit some of the classes being offered on campus. I clearly remember aspects of two of the classes I visited. However, one class in particular struck me in a significant manner. The course dealt with systematic theology and was taught by Southern Baptist professor of theology, the late Dr. Bill Hendricks. He looked out at a huge classroom of easily over a hundred students and pointedly asked this far-reaching question to all and each of us: "What is most important? What is most important in life? Is it being, doing, having, or knowing?" He paused and repeated the questions: "What is most important? What is most important in life? Is it being, doing, having, or knowing?" Then he said, "Let's look at Jeremiah 9:23–24." It reads,

> Thus says the LORD: Let not the wise man boast in his wisdom, let not the mighty man boast in his might, let not the rich man boast in his riches, but let him who boasts boast in this, that he understands and knows me, that I am the LORD who practices steadfast love, justice, and righteousness in the earth. For in these things I delight, declares the LORD.

Dr. Hendricks then explained the text by saying, "When the trials come—like in Jeremiah's day, in which Israel was going to lose everything—being wise will not help. A strong military and national power will be useless. Having possessions will be worthless. There will be only one thing that matters and that one thing is knowing—knowing God." He continued, "I can prove that knowing is most important in life by looking at the definition of eternal life. Turn to John 17:3. 'And this is eternal life, that they know you the only true God, and Jesus Christ whom you have sent.'" Dr. Hendricks was expounding upon a great truth, a truth that we simply overlook on a constant basis as we live out our lives. We are placed here on this planet to know God. We are not to focus on our being, or our experience and self-esteem, nor on our doing, or activities and accomplishments, nor on having possessions or material goods, but we are to focus on our relationships, first and foremost our relationship with God.

KNOWING GOD

What does it mean to know God? As we look at Jeremiah 9:23–24, we see that the passage speaks of boasting in both "understanding" and "knowing" God. These two words provide us with a full-orbed definition of what it means to know God, and also helps us to answer the question, "Do I love God?" The Hebrew word for "understand" is *sakal*. It speaks of the *cognitive* domain of learning, i.e., one is able to boast in the reality that she knows *truth about* God. The facts about the true and living God (as opposed to false, contrived, and imaginary gods) are crucial to faith, especially in the midst of a trial. Knowing about God comes primarily from the Scriptures. How great is your God? The Westminster Confession of Faith synopsizes the greatness of our God in chapter 2, "Of God, and of the Holy Trinity," where it is written (get ready for some heavy and thoughtful stuff),

1. There is only one living and true God, who is infinite in being and perfection. He is a most pure spirit, invisible, with neither body, parts, nor passive properties. He is unchangeable, boundless, eternal, and incomprehensible. He is almighty, most wise, most holy, most free, and most absolute. He works all things according to the counsel of his own unchangeable and most righteous will, for his own glory. He is most loving, gracious, merciful, long-suffering, abundant in goodness and truth, forgiving iniquity, transgression, and sin, and he is the rewarder of those who diligently seek him. He is also most just and terrifying in his judgments, hating all sin, and will by no means acquit the guilty.

2. God has all life, glory, goodness, and blessedness in and of himself. He alone is all-sufficient, in and to himself, not standing in need of any creatures which he has made, nor deriving any glory from them, but rather manifesting his own glory in, by, to, and on them. He alone is the fountain of all being, of whom, through whom, and to whom are all things. He has absolute sovereignty over them, to do by them, for them, or upon them whatever he pleases. In his sight all

things are open and manifest; his knowledge is infinite, infallible, and independent of his creatures; so that nothing to him is contingent or uncertain. He is most holy in all his counsels, in all his works, and in all his commands. To him is due from angels and men, and every other creature, whatever worship, service, or obedience he is pleased to require of them.

3. In the unity of the Godhead there are three persons, of one substance, power, and eternity: God the Father, God the Son, and God the Holy Spirit. The Father is of none, neither begotten nor proceeding; the Son is eternally begotten of the Father; the Holy Spirit eternally proceeds from the Father and the Son. (1993 Modern English Study Version)

These three paragraphs contain one of the greatest summaries of the nature and character of the God of the universe ever composed by human authors. There is no other god like the triune God who reveals himself in Scripture. Theologians can study, analyze, research, meditate upon, teach, and try to explain the greatness of God but, for both them and the believer in Christ, understanding God is never fully complete. Nevertheless, as people and followers who are devoted to what is indeed most important, we seek to understand everything we can about God. All Christians are theologians, i.e., God-studiers or students of the Divine! What is most important—what do we boast (or rely upon) in the tough times? That we "understand" God. This involves proper head knowledge and learning about God from the revelation of himself in Scripture, Christ, and nature. So, how great is your God?

One of the most stirring stories of the founding of Reformed Theological Seminary (RTS) involved its first president, Dr. Sam Patterson. Dr. Patterson eventually became convinced that, because none of the Southern Presbyterian seminaries in the early 1960s would affirm that the Bible was the infallible and inerrant Word of God, the creation of a new seminary that would train Bible-believing pastors and missionaries was indeed needed. Dr. Patterson decided to take his vision to some laymen who might possibly be interested in the creation of a new seminary. The first layman that he met with was a friend of his, Mr. Erskine Wells. They had known each other for a number of years and shared a mutual fondness for one another. When they met, however, Sam was all business and Erskine knew that he had something serious on his mind. Sam Patterson began to lay out a vision for the beginning of a biblical seminary to serve their denomination. Erskine listened attentively and then Sam laid out his challenge, "Erskine, I want *you* to help me to do it!"

Erskine was incredulous, telling Sam that it was a ridiculous idea. He stated to Sam, "We have no land, no buildings, no money, no library, no faculty, and no students. It is completely out of the question." Erskine Wells expected Sam Patterson to be surprised at his reaction and to back down from the suggestion. However, with great resolve, while staring Erskine Wells straight in the eyes, Dr. Patterson asked him, "Erskine, how big is your God?" Hearing this direct question in the context of the conversation, Erskine Wells replied, "When do we start?"[1] In this act of unreasonable faith in a very big God, RTS was begun. And over the years the founders watched God put the hand of his blessing upon the school, growing and expanding it in their time. I personally met with Erskine Wells when we dedicated the RTS Charlotte campus in 1997 and he was visiting for this grand occasion. He was then eighty years old. I turned to him, welcoming him to the campus. He paused. Tears welled up in his eyes, and with a gleam of joy in his glistening eyes he humbly and quietly said, "We never thought that God would do anything like this!" How big is your God? The depth of your love for God is often experienced in proportion to your understanding of who and how great he is!

In addition to the importance of "understanding" God, however, we notice that Jeremiah includes an additional concept: "but let him who boasts boast in this, that he understands and *knows* me" (Jer 9:24, emphasis added). The Hebrew word for "know" is *yadah. Yadah* speaks of intimate and experiential knowledge of God, a knowledge that goes beyond merely understanding who God is. It would be one thing to be able to quote the entire Westminster Confession's definition of God above by memory; it is

1. Hobbs, *How Big Is Your God?*, 199.

another matter to be able to say, "I have seen this great God working in my life, answering my prayers, and showing me his glory in
daily life. I personally have experienced the great and wonderful
God of the universe intervening in my own life. I know him!" Such
a vibrant and real experience of the living God is an elusive and
foreign concept to many people. God may be "there," (reigning
over the vast universe), but he isn't "here" (moving in my own life,
close to me and touching my heart).

SUBSTITUTES GET IN THE WAY

Although knowing God personally is ultimately a blessing granted
by a God who is pleased to graciously reveal himself to us, we often
create our own impediments in regard to fully enjoying God. The
late Andrew Murray, Jr. (1828–1917) writes,

> The question comes again: "Why is it that God's people
> do not know their God?" And the answer is: They take
> anything rather than God—ministers, and preaching,
> and books, and prayers, and work, and efforts, any ex-
> ertion of human nature, instead of waiting, and waiting
> long if need be, until God reveals Himself.[2]

Andrew Murray's background was influenced by what is
known as the "deeper life" or Keswick camp. The Keswick move-
ment is an evangelical tradition that emphasizes God's work in the
heart, as opposed to becoming consumed by the "doings" and "activities" of Christian faith. By "waiting" on God, I believe he means
listening, being quiet in his presence, meditating on Scripture and
seeking a God who will reveal himself to those who earnestly seek
him. He was hoping for personal revival in the soul of the believer.
The question remains, "Do I love God?" The evidence that we love
anyone is seen by the personal devotion and time we spend with
them in loving interaction and communion.

What is most important in life? About what must a person boast when everything conceivably is taken away from her?

2. Murray, *Master's Indwelling*, 18.

Understanding *who* God is and what he is like and *knowing* him in a real and personal way is the answer! Do I love God? Understanding and knowing him is what loving God means! And we find this love by receiving Christ into our lives. We become adopted children who obtain intimate freedom with their loving father. "But to all who did receive him, who believed in his name, he gave the right to become children of God" (John 1:12). The two seminaries that trained me personally underscore what is most important in life through their simple mottos. Columbia International University of Columbia, South Carolina, created the memorable motto, "To Know Him and to Make Him Known," while Reformed Theological Seminary's motto is "A Mind for Truth and a Heart for God." Either would provide a great motto for a believer's life.

QUESTIONS FOR REFLECTION

1. How do we express the focus of "being," "doing," or "having" domains in our personal lives or in our culture? Compare and contrast them. What are some examples in day-to-day life?

2. Why do these three emphases (being/doing/having) compete so strongly with our love for (i.e., knowing) God?

3. Why do we so easily create idols (i.e., substitutes) for God in our lives? What are some of our idols? What do idols do to us and how do they influence our relationship with God?

4. Name a couple of the attributes of God from the list in the Westminster Confession of Faith mentioned in the chapter that made an impression on you. In what ways do those specific attributes make God "bigger" to you?

5. How does the reality of a *big* God affect your Christian life?

6. Why does it seem easier to "understand" who God is (or learn facts about God) than it is to "know" (build intimacy with) God personally? How do we go from understanding to knowing God?

ACTION POINTS

1. Make a list of four or five attributes of God that you want to study further. Find a book like *Knowing God* by J. I. Packer, *The Knowledge of the Holy* by A. W. Tozer, *The Attributes of God* by A. W. Pink, or *The Existence and Attributes of God* by Stephen Charnock, and read further on those attributes.

2. While reading one of the books listed in Action Point 1 above, commit yourself to taking three to five minutes to simply dwell upon and pray about the specific attribute of God that you just encountered.

PRAYER

"Create in me a clean heart, O Lord, and renew a right spirit within me (Ps 51:10). Help me to see all of the competing priorities that keep me from making you first in my life. Convict me of those sins that I cherish too dearly and grant me a spirit of repentance so that I might follow you with my all. Show me your glory that I may fall humbly before you, acknowledging that you are the one who sustains me at all times and that you are deserving of my worship and submission. I need your Holy Spirit to work in my heart and make me fully yours. In Christ's name I pray, amen."

Chapter 3

The Three Domains of the Heart

A man may be theologically knowing and spiritually ignorant.

Stephen Charnock

Let us cleave to Christ more closely, love Him more heartily,
live to Him more thoroughly, copy Him more exactly,
confess Him more boldly, and follow Him more fully.

Bishop J.C. Ryle

KNOWLEDGE AND EXPERIENCE

There are many things in life that I have read about, heard stories about, or watched through the means of television or a video source of some sort, but have personally never done or experienced. As a young teenager, with awe and amazement, I saw a man step on the surface of the moon. Unbelievable. But personally, I have never even entered a space ship. I have watched many videos of people bungee jumping off of almost every conceivable starting point, from bridges, constructed platforms, and dams to cliffs and skyscrapers. But, as much as I might be tempted to do so, I have never personally bungee jumped from anywhere. And I probably never will! I have watched baseball pitchers throw a ball over a hundred miles per hour, including seeing the fastest recorded pitch ever in a Major League Baseball game on live television. That pitch was thrown by Aroldis Chapman, at that time of the Cincinnati Reds, and was clocked at 106 miles per hour (and it was an inside pitch—think about that!). I've hit in batting cages in which the ball is thrown at 80 miles per hour—there's no comparison and I can only imagine 106. There are a lot of things I have seen done but have not personally experienced—the list could be exhaustive.

Therefore, as we approach this chapter, I need to ask some other thought-provoking questions: "Can one *know* something without experiencing it?" and, "Can we separate knowing *about* (or understanding, i.e., intellectual knowledge) from knowing *through* the channel of *experience*?" That is, does cognitive or head knowledge suffice in itself without a personal experience related to that knowledge? To put it in scientific terms, does knowing about all of the chemical reactions that might occur between various substances when mixed equate to entering the lab and experiencing the mixing of those substances and watching the changes and reactions occur in a laboratory experiment? I would tend to say that the first position involves "book learning," while the other demonstrates hands-on, visible, and actual learning. One is *knowing about*, while the other is *knowledge gained through experience.* The old Puritan tradition viewed the Christian life as "experimental," i.e., they meant that it was experiential or experienced. Living for Christ did not involve simply hearing the truths of Scripture when they were taught, as well as growing in knowledge, but in experiencing the Christian life. Christ must be real to the believer and the Holy Spirit must be actively working in the heart and life of the believer.

So, I continue this thought—can real knowledge be gained without experiencing the realities and implications of that knowledge? I would like to contend that, hypothetically and theoretically, it seems that it can be; yet, truly I believe that we cannot fully know without experience. Experience equals knowledge, but knowledge (learning) does not always equal experience. At the time of this writing, I have known my wife for almost forty years.

We have been married close to thirty-eight years. I know her but I have also experienced life with her. Ours has been a walk through life together. Some years ago, when my mother-in-law moved out of her longtime home, I went through numerous photo albums that the family had saved over the years. I found many photos of my wife taken during her childhood. When looking at some of these photos, I often think, "What would it have been like to have known her in elementary or high school?" I can only imagine those scenarios and imagination takes me nowhere. The reality is that I did not experience my wife in any way until I met her one day on a sidewalk on the way to a chapel service during my first year of seminary. We were both twenty two years of age. Yet, even then, although I had met her and knew her by name, I did not "experience" her until a year had passed by. It took persistence on my part because she rebuffed my multiple efforts to date her for a number of months. Finally, she showed mutual interest in pursuing the relationship and in two months we were engaged (not recommended). Six months later, we were married.

Finally, then, I would not only know her by name and appearance, I would *personally experience* knowing her and would do so in ways beyond description. We have lived together, moved together, taken risks together, watched God work in us together, suffered setbacks together, had and raised children together, grieved over dying parents together, done ministry together, and our lives have been a series of knowing each other through literally thousands of shared experiences. And I can't think of having a better partner with whom to share (or experience) life together. Even on our thirtieth anniversary some years ago, we both learned new things about each other's lives. We continue to "experience" each other, taking the "knowing" of each other to a higher level, one of the blessings of a lengthy marital relationship. So, I do believe that we cannot know something or someone factually until we can know it or them experientially. This premise will help us understand how to answer the question, "Do I love God?"

KNOW, FEEL, DO

Years ago, as I finished up a Bachelor of Arts degree from the Arnold School of Public Health and Health Education at the University of South Carolina, I took a senior course on "Teaching Methodologies." It was a small class of students designed for upperclassmen in our major and there were not many of us attending the course at that time. Almost everything we did could be deemed as small group teaching. Most of the course was taught in a lecture format but near the end of the semester the professor decided to get this small group (less than ten students) to debate an issue which was on his mind and, I'm sure, part of his lesson plan. The matter was truly one dealing with educational philosophy and it addressed the teaching/learning process on its most elementary level. Seating us in a small circle, my professor asked the group this question: "How do you know when a person has truly learned something, i.e., when do you, the teacher, know that *true* learning has taken place?" He went on to clarify the question: "How do you know when a person has truly learned something? Is it changed *knowledge*, changed *attitude,* or changed *behavior*? Let the discussion begin." And so it did.

How would you answer? This question is a tough one because in reality there is no correct answer. However, the professor pitted us against each other and, surprisingly, among the three possible answers, I was all alone both with my answer and its defense. All three answers had proponents. I was the only one in the entire class who said that true learning has taken place if *knowledge* has changed. *Attitude* had a handful of advocates and *behavior* produced a strong group of defenders as well. The question wasn't so much a trick question as it was an avenue to see what type of outcomes an aspiring teacher would be seeking in the process of education. Eventually, and to my surprise, after much discussion and debate, the teacher relented and took my viewpoint and agreed with me. At least he granted that there was validity to my position. And why did he do that? My concluding argument was actually based on my Christian worldview (although I didn't even know what a Christian worldview was, by definition, at that time).

I built my case on the need for truth in education. I explained that if the learner was receiving wrong or false teaching, true learning would never take place, even if either attitude or behavior had been changed. My final point of illustration was that if a parent believed that giving candy to a newborn infant was the proper means to help the baby eat and grow, the baby would miss out on all of the necessary nutrients for developmental growth. No one debated me on that point. The professor agreed, although he did say that studies had proven that eventually the baby wouldn't want candy anymore (Who did that study? "No babies were harmed in this experiment!"). My premise was that correct knowledge was preeminent in the education process. I guess that I was right in my assumption and yet I guess that no one in the class was completely correct. Nevertheless, of course, we discovered that all three options presented by the professor are crucial to true learning.

A few years passed and I attended and then graduated from seminary. Immediately after seminary, I began doing campus ministry at the University of Florida. Our ministry quickly affiliated with Reformed University Fellowship (RUF) and, due to this connection, I began to attend RUF staff training at the Reformed Theological Seminary (RTS) campus located in Jackson, Mississippi. One of the RTS professors at that time was Dr. Paul Kooistra, who taught education courses, among others. He sat down with a few of us campus ministers for lunch one day in an informal setting on campus underneath a tree outside the classroom building. We talked about counseling. In the most simple but profound manner possible, Dr. Kooistra summed up the ministry of counseling as the ability of the counselor to discern a person's mind, emotions, and behavior regarding the issue with which he is dealing. We want the person in counseling to tell us three things: 1) what he thinks or believes; 2) how he feels about his beliefs; and 3) how he acts upon his beliefs. Dr. Kooistra said that, biblically speaking, the heart, or the entirety of the person, is expressed by these three domains: thinking, feeling, and doing. Counseling is founded upon changing the heart, which means that we must discern what people believe, how they feel about their beliefs, and how they live out their beliefs, as well as the decisions they will make based upon their beliefs and emotions.

THE THREE TESTS OF 1 JOHN

These three heart domains mentioned by Dr. Kooistra reminded me not only of my Teacher/Learner education course I had taken as a senior at USC, but also brought to memory similar concepts I encountered some months after graduating from college. Just before attending seminary in 1977, I had to live at home with my parents while awaiting knee surgery on a chipped kneecap I had injured a few years earlier. I spent the spring of 1977 recovering from knee surgery, while at that time substitute teaching and, in my free time, studying the book of 1 John. For some reason, I became enamored by this short and simple epistle. As I studied the book, I discovered that 1 John, in emphasizing the need for assurance of salvation, laid out three tests that determine whether or not an individual is a true believer. These three tests were:

1. The doctrinal test—or, "What do you believe (in this case, about the Messiah)?"

2. The social test—or, "How do you love others?"

3. The moral test—or, "How do you live in regard to sin and righteousness?"

These three tests, or themes, are interwoven throughout the book, appearing and reappearing in repetitive cycles. The three tests reflect the learning domains mentioned above: truth, or the cognitive domain (doctrinal test); love, or the affective domain (social test); and righteousness, or the behavioral domain (moral test). The Apostle John, who writes the book, is dealing with an early, pre-Gnostic heresy that had entered the church in the first century. Adherents to this heresy were proclaiming two things: 1) that Jesus wasn't truly God in the flesh, therefore, he wasn't the Messiah (some said his appearance was ghostlike); and 2) an individual's spirit is separated from the flesh, therefore, one can do anything in the flesh (in essence, practice sin) and it will not affect the spirit of the person. These were troubling heresies leading the church members in that day to wonder who really was a Christian. They also needed to know how to recognize a true believer in Christ. John addresses this need for assurance—or reassurance— by pointing out the inconsistencies in the false teachers' (or false professors') thinking, as well as in their love and in their behavior. In building his case for who is in Christ (assurance), he also builds a case for who is *not* a true believer (discernment). We will briefly consider each "test," understanding that the book of 1 John assists us in answering the question, "Do I love God?"

Rather than analyze or outline the book (which I also did in 1977), I want to briefly demonstrate how John poses the three tests throughout the book.

TEST #1: TRUTH—THE DOCTRINAL TEST

John buttresses the doctrinal test ("What do you believe?") by using the following terminology regularly in the epistle: "commands," "know/known," "acknowledge," "the Word of God," "the will of God," "teach," "promise," "belief," "believe," "testify," and "testimony." All of these terms refer to the concept of God's truth and the need for orthodox belief, particularly about Jesus. The person who claims to be a follower of Christ must confess the Son and believe the testimony of the Father. The Messiah has come in the flesh and true believers will acknowledge this reality. Chapter 4 of 1 John begins:

> [1] Beloved, do not believe every spirit, but test the spirits to see whether they are from God, for many false prophets have gone out into the world. [2] By this you know the Spirit of God: every spirit that confesses that Jesus Christ has come in the flesh is from God, [3] and every spirit that does not confess Jesus is not from God.

Do I love God? Only if I believe in Christ, who is the eternal Son incarnate in the flesh, sent by the Father to satisfy God the Father's wrath upon our sins (known as the doctrine of "propitiation"), and not for ours only but for those of the whole world (1 John 2:2). That is the doctrinal test, in brief. *But this test is not alone.* There are two other proofs of faith.

TEST #2: LOVE—THE SOCIAL TEST

The second domain of assurance is the social test, the test of love. It asks and answers the question, "How do you love?" The Apostle John is quite clear in chapter 2:

> [9] Whoever says he is in the light and hates his brother is still in darkness. [10] Whoever loves his brother abides in the light, and in him there is no cause for stumbling. [11] But whoever hates his brother is in the darkness and walks in the darkness, and does not know where he is going, because the darkness has blinded his eyes.

Laying down our lives for others and actively providing for those in need are marks of the true believer. Love fulfills the commandment given by God. Chapter 3 states, "Whoever does not love abides in death. Everyone who hates his brother is a murderer, and you know that no murderer has eternal life abiding in him" (vv. 14b–15). Do I love God? When it comes to others, whom do I love, how do I love them, and, conversely, whom do I treat with hate?

TEST #3: RIGHTEOUSNESS—THE MORAL TEST

The third test is the moral test or the test of "life" or lifestyle. This test answers the question, "How do you live?" That is, is your life one that reflects scriptural obedience and righteousness? The true follower of Christ follows the one who both declared, "I am the light of the world" (John 8:12) and told his followers in the Sermon on the Mount, "You are the light of the world!" (Matt 5:14). The Apostle John uses multiple phrases to develop this third test of assurance throughout the book: "righteousness/right/righteous," "unrighteousness," "darkness," "sin/sinning," "obey/obedience," "commands," "light," "purify/pure," and "law." He states, quite forcefully, in chapter 3

> [4] Everyone who makes a practice of sinning also practices lawlessness; sin is lawlessness. [5] You know that he appeared in order to take away sins, and in him there is no sin. [6] No one who abides in him keeps on sinning; no one who keeps on sinning has either seen him or known him.

As mentioned above, the early church to whom John wrote was experiencing false teaching that allowed believers to sin in or with their bodies, with the excuse that the flesh does not affect the spirit of the person. Instead of seeking to be Christlike, pure, and holy by living obedient lives, these early believers were being tempted (as also we are today) to live both for themselves and their fleshly (lustful) desires and passions. John writes to correct this common error. "Do I love God?" How is my holiness, my obedience, and my purity? Has anyone seen the light of Christ shining through me or is darkness pouring forth? Am I fighting sexual sin and other sinful desires and personal idols? The lover of God doesn't simply believe properly and love generously, but constantly wages battle against sinful habits and passions that war against the soul. The writer of the book of Hebrews reminds us, "Strive for . . . the holiness without which no one will see the Lord" (12:14).

To conclude this summary of the three domains of the heart in the epistle of 1 John, I will provide a very short section from chapter 2 of the letter in which John combines all three emphases:

> [3] And by this we know that we have come to know him, if we *keep his commandments (moral test)*. [4] Whoever says "I know him" but does not keep his commandments is a liar, and *the truth [doctrinal test]* is not in him, [5] but whoever keeps [*moral test*] his word [*doctrinal test*], in him truly *the love of God [social test]* is perfected. By this we may know that we are in him: [6] whoever says he abides in him ought to *walk in the same way [moral test]* in which he walked. (italics and brackets added for emphasis)

QUESTIONS FOR REFLECTION

1. What is the problem with having only "head" knowledge about another person? How does this relate to having only head knowledge about God?

2. Why is personal experience so vital in a Christian's life? What do you think of the person who says, "I'm a Christian," but has never experienced God's work in his life?

3. Which is the easiest to evaluate in another individual's life—the doctrinal test, the social test, or the moral test? Why? Which is most difficult?

4. Why is it easy to think a person is a Christian even though they only display one of the tests of assurance found in 1 John?

5. What are some false doctrines found in the Christian church today?

6. What is the church's, as we see it today, biggest failure in the "moral" or purity test of assurance?

ACTION POINTS

1. Read through 1 John and look for the three tests of assurance. Conduct a brief personal Bible study by underlining or circling the three tests as they appear in the book.

2. Write down some conclusions from the reading/study mentioned in Action Point 1 above.

3. Just for fun, find another person and ask her, "How do you know when a person has truly learned something? Is it changed *knowledge*, changed *attitude*, or changed *behavior*?"

PRAYER

"O Lord, I confess that I can so easily go through the motions of living out the Christian life, without pausing and taking serious time to contemplate who you are and to thus give you the praise and adoration you deserve. Help me to express wholehearted love to you. Remove from my heart those loves that prevent me from loving you fully. In Christ's holy name. Amen."

Chapter 4

The Three Tests—
Wholly Loving God

*There is no mistake more terrible than to suppose that activity
in Christian work can take the place of depth of Christian affections.*

THOMAS BOSTON

*If Jesus Christ be God and died for me,
then no sacrifice can be too great for me to make for Him.*

C.T. STUDD

Throughout my many years of ministry, in both campus and church settings, I discovered a deep need among those who claim to be God's people. As a matter of fact, it was a nagging fear in my own life as a young Christian, lasting over two years after I turned my life over to Christ. I have found that, whether Protestant or Catholic, committed or uncommitted, taught or untaught, many professing Christians lack assurance of their salvation. Much of this wavering is based on bad theology or poor doctrinal understanding, but feelings of guilt and inconsistency of life as well contribute to this "plague" of the soul. How many times have

I heard a person in the pew or a college student in the throes of the semester tell me, "I just don't know for certain if I am going to heaven," or "I don't always feel like I am a Christian"? Assurance of salvation, or the certainty that one is right with God and *has* eternal life, is a very important component of a victorious Christian life. Assurance is not absolutely necessary to being a Christian, but with assurance comes great joy of heart and peace of soul. Bishop J. C. Ryle once wrote, "Faith [in Christ], let us remember, is the root, but assurance is the flower."[1]

WHO LIKES TESTS?

I have never been one to love tests or the testing process. I doubt if many people do enjoy them, especially when something important is on the line! I personally carry too many bad memories of exam or test anxiety and fear of failure. Intense study and the demands upon time, energy, and memory were also discomforting to my peace of mind. I still remember taking my driver's license exam and having the attending police officer (I got the "bad" officer, according to my friends) say at the end of the driving portion of the exam, "Well, I hate to just barely pass someone, but I'm going to do it this time." As happy as I was to pass, my self-esteem did not improve much that day. I could go on about college courses with weekly tests, high school chemistry exams, math exams in the third grade, and other terrifying situations. Tests usually prove something about ourselves and often reveal our weaknesses. The results can be both intimidating as well as discouraging. Yet, tests often tell us the truth and reality of our given situation. As a professor, as much as I dislike giving (and grading to some extent) a course exam, I can discover a lot about a student when I see the end result of a semester of study (or lack of it!) on an exam. Tests do prove something! As mentioned in chapter 3, truth, love, and righteousness (or purity) are three tests that demonstrate what our Christian faith is really like. Each, according to the Apostle John,

1. Ryle, *Holiness*, 156.

are crucial to the Christian's assurance of salvation. All three of these tests—belief, love, and life—provide proof of love for God in a follower of Christ. The three tests of 1 John help us to answer the question, "Do I love God?" These three domains comprise what theologians call "the heart" of the believer. It appears that, according to the Apostle John, a person who professes to be a follower of Christ may very well not be one if he fails any of the three tests. Let's look at each test a little more closely in order to answer the question, "Do I love God?" And hopefully we will gain the joy and peace of assurance as well, while avoiding the failure that a serious, introspective test might generate. We might even reword the question in this chapter just for the sake of clarification: "Do I love God with my whole heart—mind, emotion, and will?"

TRUTH—LOVING GOD WITH THE MIND

None of us like people who lie or give false testimony, especially those who misrepresent the facts about us! What we value is truth and accuracy! As I write, there has been a huge national uproar about the use of "fake news" during the US presidential campaign. Both sides of the voting population accuse the other of espousing made up stories to influence the election. Both sides are equally appalled. If that is true for human beings, how much more when the facts are skewed or misrepresented about God!

According to the Apostle John, if an individual says he loves God but cannot define Christ according to Christ's *true* nature (the incarnate Son of God and Messiah), as revealed by Scripture, and does not humble himself before his glorious presence, he is actually pursuing a false Christ. The Apostle John emphatically declares that this person denies God the Father as well. John has no patience with such doctrinal heresy; he writes in chapter 3,

> [22] Who is the liar but he who denies that Jesus is the Christ? This is the antichrist, he who denies the Father and the Son. [23] No one who denies the Son has the Father. Whoever confesses the Son has the Father also.

Theology (or right thinking about God) matters. Bad theology demonstrates the possibility, at least, of not having the Son in one's life, no matter how he loves others or lives his life. God the Father does not allow or accept false worship, and false worship is based upon bad doctrine. John confronts the false teaching of his day with the argument that to deny Christ is also to deny the Father and ultimately not to have a relationship with the Father. To confess Christ (as the truth and the Messiah) is to have the Father. Loving God the Father is demonstrated by honoring and, in essence, worshipping his Son, Jesus Christ!

Bad theology (heresy or wrong beliefs about God and Christ) makes a person a liar and John goes so far as to declare, unequivocally, that the person with bad thinking about Jesus is guilty of having a spirit of the antichrist—a very sobering thought! Bad belief about Jesus presupposes that a person is against Christ. John argues convincingly that one's understanding of God is crucial to one's possession of God. And from John's writings, the reader would conclude that if a person does not have the Father, he does not truly or properly love God. John says it like he sees it (for his day and ours), even if it hurts. Conversely, however, on a positive note, John concludes that if you do have the Son, you have the Father. Such reassurance prompts a positive answer to the question, "Do I love God?" from the true believer: "I have the Son; thus I have the Father!" Embracing Jesus for who he is brings great assurance that the believer belongs to God.

LOVE—LOVING GOD WITH THE EMOTIONS

However, in his efforts to give his readers assurance (or discernment) about their possession of true faith in Christ, John doesn't simply stop at the doctrinal test. He adds a second test. That test, as mentioned in the previous chapter, involves the manner in which the follower of Christ *loves*. Love, of course, for many, is the defining attribute of Christian faith. People exalt the virtue of love. They do so whether or not one has saving faith in Jesus the Messiah, who came to earth and both lived and died, as well as rose again, in human flesh. The American mantra is "Love is all you need!" However, we have already seen that love is not all you need to be a genuine Christian and a lover of God. The Apostle John does indeed address the need for Christian love throughout the book. In 4:7–21 he mentions the word "love" twenty-seven times, an overwhelming emphasis, although the reader must remember that John is known as "the disciple whom Jesus loved" (John 13:21–30; 18:15–18; 19:26–27)—his writings should radiate the love of Christ.

And what do we learn about the type of love that is demanded of Christ's follower?

1. A true believer cannot practice hatred toward others. John writes in chapter 2,

> [9] Whoever says he is in the light and hates his brother is still in darkness. [10] Whoever loves his brother abides in the light, and in him there is no cause for stumbling. [11] But whoever hates his brother is in the darkness and walks in the darkness, and does not know where he is going, because the darkness has blinded his eyes.

2. A true believer lays down his life for his friends. First John 4:16 states, "By this we know love, that he laid down his life for us, and we ought to lay down our lives for the brothers."

3. A true believer cannot close up her heart toward another person in obvious need. Again, in chapter 3 he explains,

> [17] But if anyone has the world's goods and sees his brother in need, yet closes his heart against him, how does God's love abide in him? [18] Little children, let us not love in word or talk but in deed and in truth.

4. A true believer loves because she has first personally experienced God's love. First John 4 states,

> [19] We love because he first loved us. [20] If anyone says, "I love God," and hates his brother, he is a liar; for he who does not love his brother whom he has seen cannot love God

whom he has not seen. [21] And this commandment we have from him: whoever loves God must also love his brother.

5. A true believer proves his love for God by keeping his commandments. Chapter 5 of John's first epistle clearly states,

> [2] By this we know that we love the children of God, when we love God and obey his commandments. [3] For this is the love of God, that we keep his commandments. And his commandments are not burdensome.

Love must radiate out of the true Christian's life. And this love will be characterized by love for one another in God's family. Jesus declared to his disciples, "A new commandment I give you: Love one another. As I have loved you, so also you must love one another. By this all men will know that you are My disciples, if you love one another" (John 13:34–35). Nevertheless, love without a commitment to the truth of God is actually a false love. It becomes an expression of affection often flowing out of either a baseless sentimentality or reciprocal benefit. Christian love finds its source in the triune (three-in-one) nature of God—Father, Son, and Holy Spirit—who have eternally expressed love for one another. If God is not a trinity of persons, love would not have existed prior to the creation of humanity. This truth (or theology) about God is the foundation for true love—we love because he is love and has first loved us.

RIGHTEOUSNESS AND PURITY— LOVING GOD WITH THE WILL

Believing God's truth and expressing sacrificial love are powerful proofs of one's love for God. But, according to the Apostle John's first epistle, they are not enough. John will not allow the false teachers of his day to persuade Christ's followers to live lives characterized by sin, disobedience, and impurity. These traits are known by the term "unrighteousness." In his typical "black and white," "you're in or you're out," direct fashion, the Apostle John declares in the first chapter,

⁵ This is the message we have heard from him and proclaim to you, that God is light, and in him is no darkness at
all. ⁶ If we say we have fellowship with him while we walk
in darkness, we lie and do not practice the truth. ⁷ But if
we walk in the light, as he is in the light, we have fellowship
with one another, and the blood of Jesus his Son cleanses
us from all sin. ⁸ If we say we have no sin, we deceive ourselves, and the truth is not in us. ⁹ If we confess our sins, he
is faithful and just to forgive us our sins and to cleanse us
from all unrighteousness. ¹⁰ If we say we have not sinned,
we make him a liar, and his word is not in us.

John does not explain all of the details and implications of
what it means to walk in the light, but he does describe it with
phrases such as "walking in light or darkness," "not practicing the
truth," and denial of sin (implying that although believers do sin,
the false teachers do not call it sin; we must confess it). Elsewhere
in the book, John describes unrighteous living as "devil-like"
(3:8–10), and describes the true Christian life as "walking as Jesus
walked" (2:6). One cannot believe the gospel and seek to love others while simultaneously living in the practice or habit of sin. The
Apostle Paul compiles many lists of sinful behavior (1 Cor 6:9–11;
Gal 5:19–21), as does Jesus (Matt 15:18–19). Perpetual, habitual,
unrepentant sinful behavior demonstrates the absence of love
for God in even the most vocal professing Christian's life. So, the
question remains, "Do I love God?" One aspect of answering this
question centers around the matter of our lives and lifestyle—what
is our holiness like? Are we seeking purity of life in our choices and
decisions? The person who loves God wants to be like Christ and
live for the glory of the Father, at any cost.

QUESTIONS FOR REFLECTION

1. What are some of the key doctrines (biblical truths) that a
   Christian should believe or confess that would encourage assurance of salvation?

2. How do both love and obedience affect one's assurance of salvation?

3. Which of the three domains—truth (belief), love (affection), righteousness (purity of life)—do you think is most crucial to gaining assurance of salvation?

4. What are some Scripture passages that would encourage assurance of salvation?

5. How do we love God with our mind? Our emotions? Our will?

ACTION POINT

Read the Apostles' Creed below and either meditate upon or study these truths in order to encourage your trust in the Lord.

The Apostles' Creed

I believe in God the Father Almighty,
Maker of heaven and earth.
I believe in Jesus Christ, his only Son, our Lord,
who was conceived by the Holy Spirit,
and born of the virgin Mary.
He suffered under Pontius Pilate,
was crucified, died and was buried;
he descended into hell.
The third day he rose again from the dead.
He ascended into heaven
and is seated at the right hand of God the Father Almighty.
From there he will come to judge the living and the dead.
I believe in the Holy Spirit,
the holy catholic church,
the communion of saints,
the forgiveness of sins,

the resurrection of the body,
and the life everlasting.
Amen.
(Modern English Version)

PRAYER

"O Lord, thank you that I can call you *God, the Father, Almighty.*
Help me to rest in your fatherly love for me and to entrust myself
to your ever-present care. And grant me a greater faith to understand how truly great, powerful, and mighty you are and that you
will act on my behalf in my time of need. As I seek to know you
better through your Word, may your love capture me in such a way
that my whole life is an expression of humble submission. In the
name of Christ your Son, amen."

Chapter 5

The Three Domains and Christ

Question: Why was our mediator called Christ?

Answer: Our mediator was called Christ, because he was anointed with
the Holy Spirit beyond all measure. Consequently, he was set apart and
completely equipped with all authority and power to execute the offices
of prophet, priest, and king of his church, in both his humiliation and
his exaltation.

WESTMINSTER LARGER CATECHISM,
QUESTION 42 (MODERN VERSION)

What does love look like? It has the hands to help others. It has the feet
to hasten to the poor and needy. It has eyes to see misery and want. It has
the ears to hear the sighs and sorrows of men. That is what love looks like.

ST. AUGUSTINE

Our perfect model and example in all things is our Lord and
Savior Jesus Christ. In him are hidden all of the treasures of
wisdom and knowledge (Col 2:3). In his person and work we find
absolute perfection and, interestingly, we also see the balance and
expression of the three domains (know, feel, do). In this chapter,

we will consider the three domains in relationship to these three areas: the salvation that Christ provides, the nature of Christ's death on the cross, and the three offices that Christ fulfills.

SALVATION AND REDEMPTION THROUGH CHRIST

First, in regard to our salvation, we must acknowledge who Jesus is (theologians call this concept "his person"). Who Jesus is determines the nature of his work on behalf of our salvation. Further, Christ's humanity includes the obvious passion that Christ demonstrates in both coming to earth and suffering as the God-man on earth. Finally, what he "does" on behalf of his people provides both the righteousness and peace that each of us needs to stand before the gaze of a holy God.

1. The *Person* of Christ (the Theology of Christ): Without attempting to write an extensive explanation, we recognize that our view or understanding of the nature of Christ (who he is—his person) is essential to his work. Theology matters and it must be the highest priority when it comes to Jesus. Gospel theology as applied to Christ is crucial to our salvation. Comprehending the person of Jesus, God in the flesh, involves acceptance of these two cardinal doctrines: Christ's humanity and Christ's deity. Both theological concepts are necessary for our salvation to be procured. Christ must be a man in a real, fleshly human body in order to undergo temptation, in order to keep and fulfill the demands of the law, and in order to actually physically die for our sins. As a man, he lived, died, rose again, and reigns at the right hand of God the Father in a true, scarred, and pierced human body. Nevertheless, as important as his human death is, its effectiveness is negated unless he is truly God and can make atonement for the sins of the world (1 John 2:2). One man can give his life for one other person, but only God can give his life for "the world" or "the many" (Mark 10:45). Yes, theology matters and makes the difference in our eternal salvation.

2. The *Passion* of Christ (the Sufferings of Christ): As mentioned above, Christ must suffer. He is a man of sorrows and acquainted with grief (Isa 53:3). His sufferings begin at his birth, which is ignominious in every way: leaving the status of eternal glory and humbling himself, taking on human flesh, being born of a virgin and seemingly "out of wedlock," born in a stable, and born of humble parents. He comes unto his own and his own do not receive him (John 1:11). He lives a life of rejection and misunderstanding, facing both suspicion and deception by the religious authorities of his day. He is attacked by his enemies and endures plots on his life, as well as apparent loneliness. Even his disciples, in particular, misunderstand his mission and purpose. He suffers due to his perfect nature, which would include a deep awareness of sin, while he constantly associates with sinners. At times, he heals and he isn't thanked. He lives with the awareness that his death is inevitable and it looms over his mind constantly. He tells his disciples that he will be betrayed (a horrible thought to any of us) by one of his own, a personal disciple and supposed friend. He is handed over to the chief priests and scribes. He endures a mockery of a trial, one that involves false testimony against him (he who is the Truth). His disciples forsake him, and one disciple from his intimate group of three, denies him three times. Then he is condemned to death, a death that he does not deserve. He endures unbelievable injustice in the courts of law. He is delivered to an unbelieving and pagan governmental political system and is mistreated by them in numerous ways. They mock him, beat him, scourge (whip) him, and eventually crucify him on the cross, the most shameful form of capital punishment of that day. He takes the penalty of our sins upon himself—the just for the unjust—an act that is overwhelmingly unjust in its import. And yet Luke tells us, in light of all that shall come, "When the days drew near for him to be taken up, he set his face to go to Jerusalem" (Luke 9:51). Passion drives him to die on the cross for the sins of the world!

3. The *Work* of Christ (Salvation/Redemption Accomplished): Jesus enters space and time, not only to die as the God-man—our redeemer—but also that he might live under the law and fulfill the law of God. Jesus fulfills all the demands of the righteousness required by God's moral law. Being the Son of God, he is perfect and "he does all things well" (Mark 7:37). Theologians call this work "the active obedience of Christ," in the sense that he takes the demands of the moral law upon himself and keeps the law, conforming to it in perfect righteousness. This "active obedience" is consummated at the cross where Christ fulfills the penalty of the law on our behalf, i.e., experiencing a gory and bloody death, as planned by the Father. His work on earth involves a fulfilling of the law, i.e., living righteously in all ways with a willingness to submit to the penalty of the law, dying as a substitute for our sins. His act of substitution is an unbelievable work of grace on our behalf! Theologians speak of his imputed righteousness, indicating that because he has fully, completely, and perfectly kept God's law without sin, his righteousness is given to believers so that God the Father sees the perfect work of the Son on their behalf, rather than their own condemning sin. What a great work and a cause to love God!

IN RELATIONSHIP TO THE CROSS

The three domains—know, feel, do—are essential aspects to consider as one reflects upon the historical event of the death of Christ on the cross. We must learn from the cross and understand the theological significance of the cross. Yet, we must never remain unfeeling about the depth of Christ's sufferings on the cross, while always being mindful that Jesus himself calls all of his followers to carry their own cross.

1. *Study* the Cross (and its implications): We can easily look at all of the theology that surrounds the cross through words—words like "atonement," "expiation," "propitiation,"

"redemption," "justification"—because these words help us to tease out the vast and powerful meaning of the cross for the salvation of believers. Christ's death on the cross provides atonement for our sins. Atonement speaks of a sacrifice for sins that brings personal reconciliation and peace with a holy, righteous God. How beautiful is the bloody death of Christ when we realize what that death means. "Expiation" and "propitiation" are two words not found in the Bible, but they describe the atonement or how the cross has reconciled us to God. Expiation explains that God has removed or taken away our guilt and paid the penalty for our sins. Propitiation describes the new attitude that God has toward us due to his Son's death on the cross. God's wrath has been satisfied through the death of his Son and we now are able to have fellowship and be friends with God. Thoughts of the cross spawn amazement. Redemption delineates the fact that the believer has been freed or released from the bondage of sin through a payment. That payment is Christ's precious blood. Redemption means we are free from enslavement (or bondage) to sin and we are free from God's righteous judgment against our sins. Grace abounds at the cross. Finally, the doctrine of justification includes the wonderful reality that through Christ's saving work at the cross we, although still sinners in God's sight, are made righteous or guiltless before the God we have offended. All of these glorious truths have great meaning for the believer's position before a holy and righteous God. This is what we mean by the concept of "studying the cross."

2. *Feel* the Cross: Nevertheless, if we are not careful, we will spend our time studying and understanding the cross with an unfeeling faith. A. W. Tozer says it so well in his book *Pursuit of God* when he states,

> The doctrine of justification by faith—a Biblical truth, and a blessed relief from sterile legalism and unavailing self-effort—has in our time fallen into evil company and been interpreted by many in such manner as actually to bar men from the knowledge of God. The whole

transaction of religious conversion has been made mechanical and spiritless. Faith may now be exercised without a jar to the moral life and without embarrassment to the Adamic ego. Christ may be "received" without creating any special love for Him in the soul of the receiver. The man is "saved," but he is not hungry nor thirsty after God. In fact he is specifically taught to be satisfied and encouraged to be content with little.[1]

The danger—and I believe it is a real one—is that we can hold on to doctrines (as well we should, since they are precious to our souls) that give us confidence before the living God, while simultaneously cherishing the doctrines more than our relationship with God. Some seem to worship doctrine above their worship of God. The cross means everything to the Christian. The gospel is liberating. But do these doctrines *stir* our love for God? This is what I mean by avoiding the "study of the cross" alone.

As we look at the cross from the standpoint of Christ's suffering, we should be moved by his passion, self-denial, pain, and misery. We comprehend something of the wrath of God against not simply sin, but our personal sin and guilt. We see Christ's loneliness and his forsakenness by God the Father. The Apostle Paul could not escape this thought. He writes, "I have been crucified with Christ. It is no longer I who live, but Christ who lives in me. And the life I now live in the flesh I live by faith in the Son of God, who loved me and gave himself *for me*" (Gal 2:20, emphasis added). Paul could not imagine the cross without recognizing the fact that Christ died for him! Billy Graham once said, "No one can take a serious look at the cross and *not be moved*." And yet, it seems we can look at the cross and not be moved. We can wear a gold or silver cross around our neck and never think twice about the pain, misery, and bodily suffering involved in this horrendous method of capital punishment in its day. Few contemplate what it means for Christ to take our sins upon himself and to endure the punishment and wrath of God the Father, upon the Son. In some

---

1. Tozer, *Pursuit of God*, 12.

ways, such endurance is unfathomable, yet it can be contemplated, to the sorrow of our hearts.

That is what is meant by "feeling" the cross. Christ's passion becomes our passion. In 2004, actor and director Mel Gibson produced a movie called *The Passion of the Christ*. In essence, and with the exception of one line, the movie contained no content outside of subtitles written in Aramaic, Hebrew, and Latin. The unfolding drama, due to its graphic imagery, not only contained plenty of feeling, but elicited both shock and weeping from the audiences who watched it.[2] Nevertheless, audiences "experienced" the sufferings of Christ, but many walked away wondering, "What does all this mean?" Evangelical author John Piper, sensing the need for a general public understanding of the meaning of the cross, wrote a book explaining the significance of Christ's passion, *The Passion of Jesus Christ: Fifty Reasons Why He Came to Die*. Dr. Piper realized that people could "feel" the cross, but he wanted them to understand (truth domain) that the cross was not simply heavy sentimentalism. It is one thing to feel the cross; it is another to study it, i.e., to gain insight as to why Christ had to die or suffer at the Father's hands. Some would say that studying the cross leads to comprehending our justification (becoming right with God) while feeling the cross leads to comprehending our adoption (becoming children of God, assured of his affection). Both doctrines are important in answering the question, "Do I love God?"

3. *Carry/Bear* the Cross: As we consider the work of Christ on the cross, we are reminded that not only did Jesus sacrifice his life for us, but he calls each of his followers to take up their cross on his behalf. He calls seriously minded followers with these words found in Luke 9:

> [23] If anyone would come after me, let him deny himself and take up his cross daily and follow me. [24] For whoever would save his life will lose it, but whoever loses his life for my sake will save it. [25] For what does it profit a man if he gains the whole world and loses or forfeits himself?

2. Many Christians did not view the film due to objections of seeing an image of Christ portrayed. The author did not view it for these and other reasons.

When one recognizes the grace of God that is found in the blood shed by the Son of God on the cross, he recognizes that salvation by faith in Christ alone is free. But free grace always elicits a response, due to the work of the Holy Spirit. Grace produces love for others, and a true understanding of grace always results in unrestrained gratitude, a thankfulness that cannot help but be energized to serve Christ and fight sin. The Apostle Paul insightfully writes in 1 Corinthians 15:10, "But by the grace of God I am what I am, and his grace toward me was not in vain. On the contrary, I worked harder than any of them, though it was not I, but the grace of God that is with me." Paul senses that he is the greatest recipient of God's grace because he is so undeserving. Yet, God's grace could not be in vain—he works or labors harder than anyone else. Nevertheless, his effort is a credit to the grace of God in his heart and life. Understanding the cross means understanding that Jesus calls us to a life of personal self-denial, loss, and suffering for his sake. If we wish to answer the question, "Do I love God?" we need to take personal inventory regarding our active obedience to Jesus's call to his disciples to take up our cross daily and follow him.

THE OFFICES OF CHRIST

As we continue to take a closer look at the three domains, we are able to observe them in Jesus's offices, those being threefold as well: Christ as prophet, Christ as priest, and Christ as king.

1. Consider Christ as a *Prophet*: He speaks God's will and he is the Word of God himself. John begins his Gospel by declaring, "In the beginning was the Word, and the Word was with God, and the Word was God" (John 1:1). Christ himself declares that he is *the Truth* (John 14:6). The prophet of God declares, "Thus says the Lord . . . " and Christ came to teach us about his heavenly father (Acts 1:1) and about our salvation. As did the prophets of old, Jesus comes to denounce sin and to call God's people to repentance and faith (Mark 1:14–15). His final prophetic words are some of the most powerful that he ever utters

and describe his priestly work: "It is finished" (John 19:30). In his prophetic role, Jesus declares the wonderful doctrine of the forgiveness of sins, due to the shedding of his precious blood. Those three words can heal the broken soul!

2. Reflect upon Christ as a *Priest*: He demonstrates passion and mercy on behalf of his people and sacrifices himself on the cross, satisfying divine justice by taking the penalty of the law upon himself. Calvary is a picture of God's infinite love on behalf of his people. The high priest in the Old Testament sacrificial system would enter into the holy of holies of the tabernacle once per year and offer a sacrifice on behalf of God's people for the covering of their sins. However, Christ offers himself on the cross as an infinite, perfect, and final sacrifice delivered to the heavenly holy of holies, in the presence of God the Father. His shed blood is the provision that takes away the sins of God's people. The writer of the book of Hebrews describes Christ's priestly work very well when he writes,

> [26] For it was indeed fitting that we should have such a high priest, holy, innocent, unstained, separated from sinners, and exalted above the heavens. [27] He has no need, like those high priests, to offer sacrifices daily, first for his own sins and then for those of the people, since he did this once for all when he offered up himself. [28] For the law appoints men in their weakness as high priests, but the word of the oath, which came later than the law, appoints a Son who has been made perfect forever.

In his priestly role, Christ reconciles sinners to God and continually intercedes for his people, providing both hope and comfort for them.

3. Contemplate the role of Christ as a *King*: He is the "Ruler of Righteousness" who calls us to obedience and who claims lordship over all of our life. Jesus is a reigning king who has conquered sin and Satan, our great enemies. And he has sent the Holy Spirit to us in order to help us conquer our daily sins. "In Christ," we are victors over sin, death, and hell! In

the book of Revelation, the Apostle John declares, "They will make war on the Lamb, and the Lamb will conquer them, for he is Lord of lords and King of kings, and those with him are called and chosen and faithful" (17:12). Similarly, the Apostle Paul writes, ". . . which he will display at the proper time—he who is the blessed and only Sovereign, the King of kings and Lord of lords" (1 Tim 6:15). As king, Christ calls out a people for himself, rules over his church, and governs them through their appointed leaders and proper church discipline, while preserving them in temptation and suffering. And as the only wise sovereign and judge, he promises to take vengeance upon his enemies.

In conclusion, as prophet, Christ speaks creation into being, provides the law to us, is the Word incarnate, and is God speaking to and guiding us. As priest, Christ fulfills the ceremonial law and sacrifices his blood on behalf of his people, while also praying for his own. As king, he rules over us, calls us to obedience, and helps us to live out the law through the power of the Holy Spirit, whom he sends to live within us.[3]

A DAILY PURSUIT

"Do I love God?" The disciple who loves God must be a person who is walking with Jesus daily through life. That is to say, the disciple must know Christ personally, not simply by mere profession of faith, but in an active, vibrant relationship in which Christ is very real and present to the follower. Is this you? Are you looking to Jesus each day in order to listen to him, respond to and follow him with your whole heart? Granted, there are always failures and lapses in our efforts to walk with Christ, and sin can enter in as well. But are you moving forward? Are you repenting of your

---

3. Rather than expound further on these three offices of Christ, I would like to recommend the following work in this regard: *Prophet, Priest, and King: The Roles of Christ in the Bible and Our Roles Today*, by RTS Charlotte Old Testament professor Dr. Richard P. Belcher Jr.

nagging, persistent sins? Are you looking to Jesus for his help and presence and do you sense his nearness even when you sometimes feel far from him? Is Jesus both your Lord and friend in your personal walk through life? He is your friend always and, thankfully, although we might love Jesus very imperfectly as we walk with him, he loves us in spite of ourselves and promises to remain faithfully by our side even in the midst of our struggles. Here is another great reason to love God—he always loves us!

QUESTIONS FOR REFLECTION

1. What great doctrinal truths about the cross stir your love for God? Consider the doctrines of atonement, expiation, propitiation, substitution, adoption, redemption, and justification as defined in this chapter. What do they mean in your life?

2. Why do believers become jaded about the death of Christ on the cross? What factors in our lives tend to make the cross less meaningful to us? Why do we forget the cross?

3. How do Christ's sufferings encourage you in living the Christian life?

4. In what ways might today's Christian "carry his cross" in daily life?

ACTION POINTS

1. Read Matthew 26:30—27:56 slowly, noting or underlining all of the different ways that Jesus suffered. Meditate upon the depth of his suffering and ask the Lord to grant you a sense of sorrow for your sins.

2. Read Isaiah 53, noting the predicted sufferings of Jesus written seven plus centuries prior to Christ's first coming. Reflect on the lowliness of Christ in his humanity and spend some time in grateful praise.

3. Find the classic hymns "O Sacred Head Now Wounded," written by Bernard of Clairvaux, or "Hallelujah, What a Savior (Man of Sorrows)," authored by Philip Bliss, and sing (or meditate on) either or both in a quiet, somber, and worshipful spirit, grateful for the cross of Christ.

PRAYER

"O Lord, as I face this day, I want to do so in the power of your Holy Spirit. I give and dedicate this day to you and thoughtfully pray this prayer: 'To see thee more clearly, love thee more dearly, follow thee more nearly' throughout the day. May it be so. 'May the mind of Christ my Savior live in me from day to day, by His love and power controlling all I do and say.' 'Be thou my vision, O Lord of my heart; naught be all else to me, save that thou art; thou my best thought, by day or by night, waking or sleeping, thy presence my light.' Amen."

from school and take my brother, me, and one of our childhood friends over to the crowd.

When we arrived, the city was stirring with people, traffic, campaigners, and every generation of onlookers possible. The crowd was vast and full of strangers, but my mother let us out of the car in order to wander into the teeming throng. It was a different day then—she just let us go! The side streets were overrun with people and it appeared that the motorcade was approaching the intersection of our side street. I've always been rather aggressive and also, being a little guy, I could squirm my way through the crowds. So, on this day, sensing that I might not really see anything at all unless I pushed my way through the masses of people, I began to meander through the various bodies crammed together like sardines. Finally, I found myself on Main Street, viewing red, white, and blue banners and streamers hanging from various buildings and windows. Not only that, but I was only a few feet away from Nixon's own presidential motorcade automobile. He was actually shaking the hands of people who were reaching out to him, extending himself out of this convertible vehicle.

I knew that this moment was my opportunity for an encounter of a lifetime. I reached out my hand like the others around me but, being a little guy in the vast horde of people, I was easily overlooked. So, I took matters into my own hands (literally). In both frustration and hope, I reached out and pulled on the front of Mr. Nixon's coat, attempting to get his attention. It didn't work. The only attention that my gesture garnered was that of a male Secret Service agent who was attending Mr. Nixon. He was no gentleman! He quickly and firmly pushed me away, back into the morass of people and, like the process of osmosis, I somehow drifted far away from Main Street, absorbed into the nameless, faceless, raving mob that surrounded the disappearing motorcade. The opportunity was gone but the memory remaining was indelible. For me, this was *the day* that Rod Culbertson met the future president of the United States of America, Richard Millhouse Nixon!

Now, I suppose that you might be saying to yourself, "He did not actually meet Richard Nixon that day!" or, "Richard Nixon definitely didn't meet Rod Culbertson!" And yes, you would be correct. But, I have to say that on a beautiful fall day in 1968 in my hometown of Greenville, South Carolina, I had an experience that I will never forget and it is a "red letter" event in my life. It is engraved on the calendar of my mind. I bring up this story because it was a big event in my childhood that still carries significance even to this day. I have described for you a memorable encounter that is etched in my mind and easily recaptured. We see something similar, but of much greater import, in the Scriptures when the Old Testament prophet Isaiah recounts his life-changing experience of meeting God.

THE DAY ISAIAH MET JEHOVAH

In Isaiah 6, the prophet recalls his own conversion to faith in the Lord as well as his calling to ministry as he writes,

> [1] In the year that King Uzziah died I saw the Lord sitting upon a throne, high and lifted up; and the train of his robe filled the temple. [2] Above him stood the seraphim. Each had six wings: with two he covered his face, and with two he covered his feet, and with two he flew. [3] And one called to another and said: "Holy, holy, holy is the LORD OF HOSTS; the whole earth is full of his glory!" [4] And the foundations of the thresholds shook at the voice of him who called, and the house was filled with smoke. [5] And I said: "Woe is me! For I am lost; for I am a man of unclean lips, and I dwell in the midst of a people of unclean lips; for my eyes have seen the King, the LORD OF HOSTS!" [6] Then one of the seraphim flew to me, having in his hand a burning coal that he had taken with tongs from the altar. [7] And he touched my mouth and said: "Behold, this has touched your lips; your guilt is taken away, and your sin atoned for." [8] And I heard the voice of the Lord saying, "Whom shall I send, and who will go for us?" Then I said, "Here I am! Send me."

The scene in these words occurs around the eighth century B.C. in the nation of Israel. The people of God have experienced some wonderful years of prosperity, luxury, peace, and political consistency under the rule of an exceptional king named Uzziah. According to 2 Chronicles 26, Uzziah had ruled the nation of Israel for fifty-two years and, in some ways, he had became a cultural icon. The people had respected him and credited him for their ability to live "the good life." The king had managed many victories over their enemies, fortified Jerusalem, had been served by massive troops (2,600 leaders commanding 300,000 soldiers), had built many impressive buildings, and had been a powerful leader of the nation of Israel. In reality, by all appearances, the people had grown dependent upon King Uzziah, trusting him for their lives and stability. And therefore, they have forgotten YHWH, the LORD.

The loss of a sense of the divine impacts Isaiah as well. When Uzziah passes away, Isaiah is shell shocked. His "god" or earthly idol has died. The "year that King Uzziah died" is not simply a chronological reference; for Isaiah, this is a "red letter" day in which his life would change—the reference to this day is intensely personal. He truly meets YHWH, the LORD, and he will never forget it, nor will he ever be the same. Isaiah goes to the temple. We are not exactly sure why he goes there. Either he goes to find relief for his grief or he is so stunned by the circumstances of this loss that he knows that he needs to find the one true God. His idol is gone. He needs to pause and to grieve. His reflection resembles the long weekend that I experienced as a child when President John F. Kennedy was assassinated on Thursday, November 22, 1963. Time seemed to stop. The trauma was deep. Very little else seemed important. Life was bigger than I was. Isaiah experiences a void in his life, an emptiness in his soul. Where is relief?

He enters the temple, and there the text tells us that he sees "the Lord" (*Adonai* in Hebrew, meaning "Master"). His vision of God is powerful. Instead of King Uzziah as his ruler, Isaiah now has a new ruler or master, as designated by the name of God, *Adonai*. Notice that the transformation of his heart and life begin with the theological (or the knowledge) domain, i.e., the knowledge of God. Isaiah experiences a personal crisis but when he sees the Lord it is his vision of God's revelation that begins the process of change.

"Do I love God?" I must answer this question by starting with another question: "What God do I see—who is God?" Isaiah gets a glimpse of the heavenly vision. Through this account, we see and learn things about the glory of our God and our Savior, Jesus Christ, that we rarely find elsewhere in Scripture and nowhere else on earth!

OVERWHELMING AWE!

As Isaiah describes this heavenly scene, he explains a vision of a great and glorious king. The Lord is on his throne. God is both judge and king. John Calvin states, "He could not have given a better description of God, in regard to place, than in the person of a Judge, that his majesty might strike greater terror into the Jews."[1] The picture of the throne is that it is "high and lifted up." The greater the king, the higher the throne. The train of the robe that this king wears fills the temple, displaying grand royalty. This is a picture of King Jesus, as John explains in his Gospel (John 12:41). It is an overwhelming scene and leaves an indelible impression on the shaken viewer.

I still recall watching what, at that time, was the most viewed wedding ever in the history of the world. This landmark wedding ceremony was broadcast on television in 1981. The late Princess Diana was marrying Prince Charles, and the latest cable technology allowed broadcast availability of this British wedding ceremony around the world. Normally, I'm not one to watch or attend a wedding unless I have to (or am officiating it), but at the time, having been married myself less than two years and hearing all of the furor over the potential pomp and circumstance of this prime-time ceremony, I actually stopped my daytime activities to watch it. I was not alone—it was termed "the wedding of the century" and was viewed by over 750 million people around the world. I don't know what others noticed most, but to me the most impressive aspect of the entire ceremony was to observe Princess Diana walk down the aisle with a twenty-five-foot-long wedding gown train. This was no ordinary Church of England wedding ceremony! The value, beauty, and

1. Calvin, *Commentaries*, vol. 7 (*Isaiah 1–32*), 201.

length of the gown was portraying elite royalty. Princess Di's apparel explains something of the great glory of the King of Israel, whom Isaiah envisions in the temple, as the train of his robe fills the temple edifice. Isaiah is contemplating elite royalty!

But the Lord is not the only presence dwelling in the visionary landscape. He is surrounded by angels—seraphs—whose very name indicates their own angelic glory. The word "seraph" speaks of fire, burning, and lightening! We can only imagine what this vision looked like as Isaiah experiences it. The angels display six wings, an unusual sight in itself. With two wings the seraphs cover their faces, demonstrating reverence, awe, and the inability—despite being sinless creatures—to look upon a holy and glorious God. With two they cover their feet, displaying both humility and modesty in the presence of God. And with two, as would be expected, they fly, portraying that they are ready to serve this great God at any moment.

And the scene doesn't stop there—it becomes filled with greater awe. These shining, radiant angels are heard crying out to one another, "Holy, holy, holy is the LORD OF HOSTS; the whole earth is full of his glory!" This repeated chorus must be staggering to Isaiah as he watches and listens transfixed with possible terror (I actually think that this worship scene is perpetual and eternal, occurring right now in heaven!) The word "holy" means, pure, clean, sacred. Theologian Louis Berkhof, quoting Lutheran scholar Rudolph Otto, states that God's holiness includes such ideas as "absolute unapproachability," "absolute overpoweringness," or "awful majesty."[2] Isaiah must be asking, "Who is *this* King?" He must be thinking, "Somehow, I've missed knowing him!" And if he is able to gather himself in any fashion, it surely doesn't last long, because suddenly the foundations of the temple thresholds begin to shake at the voice of the angel who is calling out the riveting holiness chorus. Everything appears to be falling apart in the life of Isaiah, all in a moment's time. Everything is out of control!

I spent ten years living in Gainesville, Florida, home of the University of Florida, a city that I love for numerous reasons. I served as a campus minister for Reformed University Fellowship

2. Berkhof, *Systematic Theology*, 73.

(RUF) during that time. One of the pleasures of living in a city full of college students was that I could find a place to play basketball most any time after 3:00 p.m. until very late at night (I didn't play at night, however, in order to keep my wife happy and my marriage intact). In the fall of 1989, late one afternoon I went out to play at my usual outdoor court, called Littlewood. After losing a game and sitting out and waiting for the next game to be over, one of my long-time court friends engaged me in conversation. He had just returned from a business trip to San Francisco. He had been there when the great Bay Quake of 1989 struck the area, a devastating earthquake reaching 6.9 on the Richter scale and stopping the World Series between the two Bay Area teams, the San Francisco Giants and the Oakland Athletics. He told me that he had been staying in a high-rise hotel, in one of the upper-story rooms, when the quake hit. He said that his room began to sway something like a ship being tossed at sea. His body had literally been thrown back and forth across the room, despite the fact that he had attempted to grab onto any piece of furniture he could reach. He was sure he was going to die. Thankfully, he survived without injury, but he expressed relief because he knew that he had been spared. He recognized during those perilous moments that he did not have the power to save himself in that situation.

Isaiah must feel like my basketball friend, as this broken and grieving man faces what appears to be the possible termination of his life, due to being in the presence of an awesome and holy God. He experiences a total loss of control in his circumstances. In a manner like never before, he sees God for who he is—a glorious master who reveals himself as majestic royalty, revered by burning angels, and worshiped as awesomely holy. This God is a pure being who will judge those who idolize anything else. Who can survive his piercing eye of holiness? Isaiah is certain that he cannot.

I have belabored this point in order to emphasize that *understanding who God is must be the foundation for responding to God.* Knowledge of God is the fountain that flows into response. I do not think that I can overemphasize this lesson. One's theology (or doctrine) of God's being and nature (the knowledge domain) is the essential starting point for proper heart engagement and life responsiveness. The vision of God creates passion and action! "Do I love God?" Who is your God? What is he like? He reveals himself in his Word and will show himself to those who worship him in spirit and in truth. My fear is that for many who might read this book (and I most certainly include myself), the words written by British Bible scholar and author J. B. Phillips can so easily be true: "Your God is too small." A small, ineffective, passive, and human-like god is easily toyed with and readily dismissed from our lives. Isaiah's theology has been changed in overwhelming fashion. He knows him in a new manner. How will he respond?

The knowledge domain is primary when it comes to loving God. Understanding is crucial but facts alone can become cold without the "knowing" of experience. Isaiah cannot remain unmoved by his vision. His heart and his mind are dramatically impacted by the vision of God. It is so overwhelming that his inner world crashes. Here we see the affective or emotional domain in full expression. Isaiah cries out, knowing the idolatry and sin that exists in both his heart and life, declaring, "Woe is me! For I am lost; for I am a man of unclean lips, and I dwell in the midst of a people of unclean lips; for my eyes have seen the King, the LORD OF HOSTS!" Isaiah is undone by his sin. He knows that his words have betrayed him. He should be divinely executed for not exalting such a glorious and self-existent God, the God of Israel. I once heard Dr. R. C. Sproul say that Isaiah is possibly being convicted of his personal use of profanity and thus he is ashamed of his "unclean lips." That assumption may be true, however, I believe that in the presence of fiery angels crying out reverent words of holy declaration, Isaiah understands that his daily words are never so focused. His daily words and language represent his "this world" mentality and utterly fall short of the glory of God.

Isaiah recognizes not only his own sin, but the sin of God's people. He realizes that the nation of Israel has defaulted to an unholy cultural mindset. None of their words glorify God, either. The word "woe" means to wail, lament, grieve, and feel threatened. The word lost is rendered in other versions of the Bible as "undone."

It also suggests the concepts of ruin, cessation, being destroyed, or cut off. Being in the presence of a holy God has exposed Isaiah (and Israel, with whom he must identify as a soon to be commissioned prophet) as a rejected sinner whose end should be death. He is cast down with every possible desperate emotion. He is falling apart! He needs what appears to be unavailable—a means of becoming acceptable before a holy God. He is like a filthy tramp or street bum who has stumbled into a beautiful wedding ceremony. He is more than awkwardly out of place—he will be cast out! There appears to be no hope. His guilt is real and his demise is sure.

OVERWHELMING GRACE!

But all is not lost. Bottomed-out emotions can be redeemed and transformed. This only happens, however, when God intervenes. There is no human solution to Isaiah's (or our) human dilemma. Graciously, the glorious God condescends. The text tells us that God does something on Isaiah's behalf, something that Isaiah could not do for himself. One of the seraphim has gone to the altar of the temple and removed a burning coal from its midst. In an experience that is unimaginable but real, the angel flies to the devastated Isaiah and touches the burning coal to his lips. We don't know if his lips are burned or not, or if the scene is more vision than literal reality, but something real does happen. *Isaiah has his guilt taken away.* The angel says that his sins have been atoned for. The words "taken away" mean that his sins have departed, no longer to be held against him. "To atone" means to purify or purge. His unholy status before a holy God has been changed. His confession and repentance have been rewarded with forgiveness. Where is his sin? Nowhere, in God's sight! I still recall the late Dutch World War II survivor Corrie Ten Boom addressing the issue of the believer's sins by quoting Micah 7:19: "He will again have compassion on us; he will tread our iniquities underfoot. You will cast all our sins into the depths of the sea." The depths of the sea are very deep—our sins are very, very gone. Corrie Ten Boom would add, however, with a twinkle in her eye, "And the Lord puts up a sign that says, 'No fishin'." Leave those sins behind and do not dwell upon them—they are gone!

Can we grasp what has happened? Isaiah, who is ready to be justifiably destroyed, is suddenly justified (made right with God), cleansed, and lives to tell about it. The only place where we can grasp this truth—this shadow of a future reality—is to look at the cross. At the cross, we learn truth: God is holy and must judge sin; we are undone and ruined. We need grace, help, and forgiveness. We become desperate. Our affections become involved. We are not unmoved by the depth of our predicament. We feel our dilemma so deeply that our emotions disturb us without relief. Time meets eternity. The finite meets the Infinite. We are shaken to the core. And then—we look at the cross and see a Savior. It is not a seraphim who shows up; rather, it is the very Son of God who comes. It is not a coal from the altar, but a bruised, beaten, bludgeoned, pierced, and bloodied human body that is sacrificed and provides atonement. At the cross, we can hear the Father say to those who believe, "Your guilt has been taken away; your sins have been atoned for." We do not take this exchange lightly. We are amazed that anything like this could happen in our lives. We have entered the realm of grace and have begun to understand the boundless grace of God. Christ is able to wash away the filth of my sins and make me clean. The believer's emotions are engaged. As Paul writes, every true believer experiences a deep sense that Christ is the one "who loved me and gave Himself *for me*" (Gal 2:20, emphasis added).

Isaiah hears and experiences truth; he meets a previously unrecognized and unapproachable holy God. His emotions are gripped and he is personally overwhelmed by God's grace. But this temple vision does not stop there. The text tells us that the Lord (*Adonai*) says, "Whom shall I send, and who will go for us?" With this question, God presents the opportunity for the recipient of grace to demonstrate that he understands the depth of forgiveness and cleansing that he could not find elsewhere. Isaiah hears the call of God upon his life. For him, we might say that this is both the call of conversion to the Lord as well as the specific call to be a spokesman or prophet for God. This recorded event in the life of Isaiah is surely included in his written prophesy in order to demonstrate how he has become a prophet or spokesman of the living God. But for every believer who experiences the grace of God in his/her life, there is always a call to service. There is always a necessary response. There is always a sense of grateful obligation and indebtedness to God's gracious hand. The Apostle Paul recognizes the inherent power of grace when he writes, "For I am the least of the apostles, unworthy to be called an apostle, because I persecuted the church of God. But by the grace of God I am what I am, and his grace toward me was not in vain. On the contrary, I worked harder than any of them, though it was not I, but the grace of God that is with me" (1 Cor 15:9–10). Grace generates a vigorous reaction—indebted energy on behalf of a God who loves us enough to send his Son to die for us. "Do I love God?"

We cannot read the text and imagine Isaiah looking around the temple to see if anyone else might volunteer to answer this call. His affections at this moment readily influence his will. The simple answer to the question is provided: "Then I said, 'Here I am! Send me.'" Isaiah has come face to face with a holy God and lived. But not on his own accord—God has done the work to pardon him for his sin. This is grace in its fullest expression. When God reveals himself to us and then calls us to follow and serve him, the true believer humbly and willingly submits, no matter what the cost. Experiencing grace outweighs the often difficult consequences of following the Lord. Isaiah's call is quite unbelievable. He understands that God's people are just like he was prior to the vision—dependent upon other false gods, as well as being people of unholy speech. They do not worship the great and awesome God of heaven. He is told that he is going to till very dry, hard soil. Hearts will be hard and the response will be minimal. At best, any fruit will only occur late in his ministry. Someday there will be a remnant of believers as a result of his preaching and ministry. Isaiah wonders, "How long, O Lord?" The answer, although not explicitly stated in the text, is that the people will not respond for fifty years. This is Isaiah's call to ministry. Only grace—a vision of a holy God who

3. Engaged: Although obvious, this is the opposite of being disengaged. However, we recognize the "engaged" person because she is responding to God's will and Word and cannot live without it. Sometimes she is so overcome by God and his glorious being that she is seen as consumed by the things of God. Engagement is commitment.

4. Gripped: This term describes a person who has seriously received the gospel in such a way that everything in his life is motivated out of gratitude to and service of Christ. Eternity, thoughts of God, and the reality of forgiveness have captured this person's soul. I credit Dr. Archie Parrish, Presbyterian pastor and evangelist, with introducing this poignant term to me.

5. Revived: Conversion is described as the complete transformation of the believer in Christ—mind, emotion, and will. The believer is made alive to (or "revived" by) Christ and spiritual realities that he previously did not know before finding Christ. These spiritual realities are vibrant and life transforming. Personal revival means to be made alive, just as the phrase "being born again" describes being given spiritual birth from above.

QUESTIONS FOR REFLECTION

1. Why does it so often take a crisis in our lives for us to meet God in a life-changing manner?

2. What are the idols in your life that keep you from seeking or trusting in the living God?

3. Why is the revelation of God (knowledge) necessary for the proper reception (emotions) to God? How do emotions tend to affect us when our knowledge of God is defective?

4. With which of the five words above—"reflection," "contemplation," "engaged," "gripped," and "revival"—do you identify? Why?

ACTION POINTS

1. Read Isaiah 40:1–17. What does this text tell you about the greatness of God? Take some time to "behold" or meditate upon your God and worship him for who he is.

2. Find a hymnal or look up the classic hymn "Holy, Holy, Holy," by Reginal Heber, and sing this uplifting song unto the Lord.

3. Create a short written list of verbal sins that you are aware of in your life and ask the Lord to help you specifically with them.

PRAYER

"O Lord our God, you are indeed holy, holy, holy. Help me to contemplate your holiness and greatness. I cannot comprehend the beauty of your holiness but, looking into my heart, I am able to see that I am not worthy to be in your presence. Even the thought of your glorious presence staggers me, as my sins condemn me in your sight. I have been unbelieving, rebellious, questioning, and loving what is contrary to your holiness, while constantly falling short of your glory. My lips betray me and witness against me. Thank you for the cross, where, in amazing fashion, Jesus took away my sins and atoned for my guilt. May I bow in your presence and worship you. Amen."

Chapter 7

Do You Love God?
The Gospel of Grace

I felt I did trust in Christ, Christ alone for salvation, and an assurance
was given me that he had taken away my sins, even mine, and saved me
from the law of sin and death.

JOHN WESLEY

I dread mightily that a rational sort of religion is coming in among us; I
mean by it, a religion that consists in a bare attendance on outward duties and ordinances, without the power of godliness: and thence people
shall fall into a way of serving God, which is a mere deism, having no
relation to Jesus Christ and the Spirit of God.

THOMAS BOSTON

DEALING WITH DEBT

When my wife, Cathy, and I moved our family from Clearwa-
ter, Florida, to Charlotte, North Carolina, in 1994 in order to
work with Reformed Theological Seminary, we had a difficult time
finding a home. The housing market was a seller's market and, after a

few attempts at putting down offers on various homes but watching them become purchased by someone else who got there first, we finally found our present home, which we bought in three hours, hoping not to lose it to some more eager buyer. The home wasn't perfect but it was suitable and we were glad to have it. However, when it came to finding a mortgage company, that endeavor wasn't so difficult. I don't know why we used the company that we finally did find, but in time we discovered that, out of a multiplicity of mortgage companies available, ours wasn't the best company to use. They had plenty of problems and were purchased by other mortgage companies a couple of times, changing names each time.

As an example, two or three years after we bought our Charlotte home, an unusual incident with our mortgage company occurred. Late one Friday afternoon, Cathy came home and, looking at the mail, opened a letter from the company. She read it and then immediately called me. The letter contained such amazing news that I had to drive home from work to see it for myself. When I arrived, I read the letter, which also contained our most recent mortgage payment check that we had sent in (there were no electronic payments then)—*a check that was not cashed*. They had returned the uncashed check and stapled it to an attending note that stated, "Your check is being returned because . . ." The note had about six different options explaining why the company might return a check. Someone from the company had placed a big X on one of the categories for check returns and on our document the X marked the following category: "Your check is being returned because . . . your mortgage has been *paid in full*"! What??? How could this be? Was there a mistake? Did the mortgage company suddenly decide that they were going to be gracious to one of their clients? Or possibly someone who knew us and recognized that we were always living month to month, with four growing children, decided to bless us and actually paid off our mortgage! We thought, "What would it be like to be released from a thirty-year mortgage with monthly payments of just under $1,000?" We had the uncashed check in hand and that alone was a positive. We must call the company and find out more.

However, since all of this occurred on a late Friday afternoon, the company was presently closed; office hours were complete for the weekend. We would have to call them on the following Monday. It would be a long weekend as we waited. Nevertheless, we spent a lot of the time that weekend telling people what had happened. "Our mortgage has been paid! Our mortgage is gone! Could it be true?" Our friends were almost as amazed, excited, and curious as we were. Finally, Monday morning arrived. We got the kids off to school and waited for 9:00 a.m. to arrive. Cathy called the company. A very young and sweet, but seemingly inexperienced, girl answered the phone. Cathy eagerly explained to her about the letter from the company. She couldn't wait to hear the answer. The young lady said that she would have to check with someone to see what happened. Cathy waited for some time and the girl finally returned to the phone line. She said, "I'm sorry, but apparently there has been some kind of mistake. Your mortgage is not paid." What? How disappointing! We were not free from our debt, i.e., our obligation to the mortgage company. The dreaded payments would continue, as they have up until the time of this writing, and we were saddled with the awful realization that we would continue to carry the burden of this large debt.

Now I ask you: For a moment, could you feel our liberation? Could you sense the casting away of our debt and our joy of discovering that we were free from the burden of this huge personal financial strain? The thought of such a thing is so pleasant and exhilarating! In your imagination, I would venture that you have wondered what it would be like to be out from under some similar debt that you might have carried or still do carry. What if someone rescued you from your own personal financial peril or potential ruin? Who would do such a thing? How could you thank them? How would you express your sense of relief or gratitude?

Well, such is the picture of the following story in the New Testament, a narrative that we cannot fully comprehend, but if we comprehend it at all, we will be able to answer the question, "Do I love God?"

UNDERSTANDING THE GOSPEL

In this story, we will find that the essential concept to answering the question, "Do I love God?" is centered upon one's understanding of what is commonly known as "the gospel." The gospel—the good news that there is forgiveness of sin available to those who confess and repent of their sins and entrust their hearts and souls to Jesus—is the one message that, rightly understood, will transform the heart of the broken, the needy, and the indebted. The gospel includes understanding the doctrine of justification by faith alone, the reality that God has done a work on the cross that can make us right with him. Justification by faith, as Dr. Martyn Lloyd-Jones says, is a doctrine that "means the end of all thinking about ourselves and our goodness, and our good deeds, and our morality, and all our works."[1] Understanding the gospel means that the person has "come clean" before the gaze of a holy God; the gospel includes honesty, transparency, confession of sin, and repentance. Wonderfully, the gospel leads to acceptance, through the work of Christ, by a holy, sinless, and perfect God. Love for God is derived from a spirit of brokenness, a realization that you have nothing to offer God except your sin, your moral failures, and your rebellion against God's law. In order to answer the question, "Do I love God?" I must ask you another question: "Have you been broken?" The following gospel story will help you discover your answer.

In Luke 7 we see a woman who understands the gospel. Luke gives us the account:

> [36] One of the Pharisees asked him to eat with him, and he went into the Pharisee's house and reclined at the table. [37] And behold, a woman of the city, who was a sinner, when she learned that he was reclining at table in the Pharisee's house, brought an alabaster flask of ointment, [38] and standing behind him at his feet, weeping, she began to wet his feet with her tears and wiped them with the hair of her head and kissed his feet and anointed them with the ointment. [39] Now when the Pharisee who had invited him saw this, he said to himself, "If this man

1. Lloyd-Jones, *Revival*, 55.

were a prophet, he would have known who and what sort of woman this is who is touching him, for she is a sinner." ⁴⁰ And Jesus answering said to him, "Simon, I have something to say to you." And he answered, "Say it, Teacher." ⁴¹ "A certain moneylender had two debtors. One owed five hundred denarii, and the other fifty. ⁴² When they could not pay, he cancelled the debt of both. Now which of them will love him more?" ⁴³ Simon answered, "The one, I suppose, for whom he cancelled the larger debt." And he said to him, "You have judged rightly." ⁴⁴ Then turning toward the woman he said to Simon, "Do you see this woman? I entered your house; you gave me no water for my feet, but she has wet my feet with her tears and wiped them with her hair. ⁴⁵ You gave me no kiss, but from the time I came in she has not ceased to kiss my feet. ⁴⁶ You did not anoint my head with oil, but she has anointed my feet with ointment. ⁴⁷ Therefore I tell you, her sins, which are many, are forgiven—for she loved much. But he who is forgiven little, loves little." ⁴⁸ And he said to her, "Your sins are forgiven." ⁴⁹ Then those who were at table with him began to say among themselves, "Who is this, who even forgives sins?" ⁵⁰ And he said to the woman, "Your faith has saved you; go in peace."

In this dynamic text, we see a woman who has great needs discovering what it means to be accepted and forgiven by a gracious God. In the presence of a self-righteous religious leader, a Pharisee, Jesus does something remarkable: he forgives a blatant sinner's debt. Luke sets the context for the passage earlier in the chapter when he mentions that the people have recognized that Jesus is both a prophet (verse 16) and also a friend of sinners (verse 34). What a unique combination—usually a prophet would be the person speaking truth and judgment to sinners who need to turn to God, and thus he would not be seen as a sinner's friend. The story is situated in the Pharisee's home. Jesus is present by invitation. Other guests are present as well (verse 49). We must wonder: Was Jesus invited because the Pharisee, out of curiosity, wanted to speak with a prophet? Or, was Jesus instead being welcomed in a suspicious fashion, in order to be spied upon, since no true prophet would ever be known for associating with public sinners? We are not sure, but apparently Jesus can be a friend to both sinners as well as the overtly and high-mindedly religious, even though they might suspect his motives and his intentions. Jesus may have responded to the invitation with uncertainty, but he did respond. And he has come. But, this will be no ordinary meal.

While they are engaged in the cultural dining method of reclining—or almost lying down—at the low table from which they were eating, the most unusual circumstance materializes. Surprisingly, a lady of the streets (probably a prostitute) and a known "sinner" comes into the house. We might wonder how she enters at all, but we must understand that eating a meal, as was custom in that day, involved dining in an open house and was seen as a social event. One's friends would be welcomed to come and stand around, enjoying the cool breeze in the veranda and engaging in meal-time conversation. Almost anyone could "drop by" for fellowship during the meal and in this case "someone" certainly did. And this someone is very courageous, more than we might imagine. She is a notorious sinner or prostitute, a "lowly" woman, while the house belongs to a Pharisee, well known for their righteous condemnation of lowly "sinners" unlike themselves. Why is she there? Although the text doesn't explain the answer explicitly, she most certainly understands that Jesus is a friend of sinners and he offers the brokenhearted forgiveness for their transgressions. She, herself, has many.

Surprisingly, she enters audaciously, carrying a flask of very costly perfume (probably a necessity for her past profession) and visibly weeping, while also wetting Jesus's feet with her tears and wiping them with her hair. She kisses his feet and anoints them with the perfume. Wetting his feet was an act of humility, something only a servant would do. Kissing his feet was a behavior reserved only for honoring rabbis and would be very unusual behavior otherwise. Letting down her hair in public would be a shameful deed as well. Her conduct must provide the most unusual dining interruption possible and would appear quite ostentatious. The Pharisee, watching with concentrated observation, and being well aware that this woman has a reputation for sin, smugly surmises to himself, "If this man were a prophet, he would have known who and what sort of woman this is who is touching him, for she is a sinner." He is highly offended by the woman's actions. How can Jesus tolerate such behavior?

Whether it is because of his omniscience or due to his ease of reading Pharisees through various and previous encounters with them, Jesus sees right through his host. Noticing his consternation, Jesus uses the Pharisee's name, Simon. The scene is about to become increasingly uncomfortable for this staid representative of the religious establishment. The interaction reminds us of when parents must forcefully rebuke their own children when they unknowingly step out of line. Jesus tells Simon a parable about two debtors. One man's debt is equal to approximately one and one-half years' of earnings or wages (500 days' worth), while the other's debt is one tenth as large. Jesus asks an uncomfortable question: "When they could not pay, he cancelled the debt of both. Now which of them will love him more?" In polite fashion, Simon listens, wondering what might ensue. Jesus is about to teach Simon a few things: first, he not only knows about the woman, but, second, he also knows Simon's thoughts and his heart; third, he *is* a prophet, and, finally, he is more than a prophet—he is the Messiah, the one who can forgive sins!

Simon's "I suppose" answer to the question suggests a tentative indifference or a spirit of avoidance. But Jesus has a point to make. At that moment, one might surmise that Simon probably wishes *he* had another house to visit for dinner! Jesus now turns toward the woman but points the conversation directly and forcefully toward Simon. The prostitute is "Exhibit A" for the Pharisee! Ironically, she is a visual aid for a lesson on love. Jesus wants Simon to look at her with spiritual eyes, as a woman whose heart has been changed. Simon is looking at her as she had been, not as she now is! In pointed language, Jesus demonstrates the difference between Simon's heart and actions and the woman's heart and actions. Simon indeed has hosted Jesus. But his efforts have been cold, formal, discourteous, and patronizing. Simon's home is open, but his heart is not. He doesn't love Jesus, and his suspicious spirit proves his failed attempt at a bogus hospitality. We learn from this encounter that one can look like he has received Christ into his world and life while not actually loving him. We can appear hospitable to Christ while at the same time we are not trusting him at all.

A MUCH-NEEDED DECLARATION

Jesus, in no uncertain terms, tells Simon that his love for him, as his guest, is little. As a matter of fact, the woman's overt and excessive expressions of love are overwhelming proof of the reality of her personal experience of forgiveness and love. The reality of faith is shown by one's actions and this woman believes not only that Jesus is the Messiah who forgives, but that he has forgiven her, a woman with sins beyond number. The woman has shown lavish love to Jesus, a love born out of unbelievably deep gratitude. Jesus acknowledges both her faith and her love and, based on this expressive faith, before a watching and probably suspicious gathering of guests, makes a bold declaration: "Your sins are forgiven." I must say that simply reading these words in this context is a staggering thought. Apply them to your own life. What have you done to disobey God? How have you sinned against a holy God? How have you broken God's law and hurt yourself or others? If we are honest with ourselves, the list is endless. If we see our need to run to Jesus, we are the woman in the story!

"Do I love God?" We can only answer this question by asking ourselves, "How much has God forgiven me?" "How much have I sinned against God?" "How often have I hurt others?" "How frequently do I seek my own way?" "How have I failed to love God with my whole heart, mind, soul, and strength?" "What do my words say about my relationship to God?" "How have I damaged others in my speech or actions?" "How have I failed to do what is right?" "What about my sexual addictions and sins?" "How have I lied, cheated, stolen, or deceived?" "Do my life and my words demonstrate slander, prejudice, gossip, anger, and profanity?" "Is there murder in my heart toward anyone?" The list can go on and on. Can I say, "Today, am I aware of the fact that I drove Christ to the cross and that my sins caused his death. He died for me but also because of me"? Do we, in any way, feel the depth of our sins and the death of the Savior on the cross? Or have we become too jaded to the greatest act of history? Do I recognize that Christ came and died *for me*!? The prostitute does; the Pharisee does not.

Luke tells us that the onlookers, i.e., the guests at the table, begin to interact with each other, discussing this bold declaration of Jesus's forgiveness of the woman's sins. Not only does it appear impossible for such a woman to be forgiven of her sins, but who is this Jesus that *he* is able to forgive anyone's sins? They probably know Jesus by reputation and possibly by rumor, but they never expected him to be so bold as to declare forgiveness for any sinner, much less for such a sinner as her. The truth of the matter is that this woman has been saved. She has been delivered from herself and the demons of guilt and shame plaguing her life. Her transparency about her transgressions has led her to an extreme and unembarrassed transparency of love for Jesus. Before the eyes of all the doubters, skeptics, and questioning guests, Jesus commands the woman, "Go in peace." Jesus declares not only that is she a woman of faith but that, because of her faith, she has obtained peace. Hers is a peace of heart, of mind, and of soul. It is a peace that flows from believing in Christ. She is now free. She has had her sins forgiven. The slate is clean. This unbelievable reality has led her to a love that defies description. Faith, love, and peace—these three are companions in the gospel. Gospel understanding brings peace to our lives and a flowing love from our hearts.

SEARCHING QUESTIONS

"Do I love God?" "Do I understand the gospel?" "How deep are my sins?" "How big is my debt?" "How holy is my God?" "How great is my need?" "How broken is my heart?" "How endangered is my soul without the intervening grace of God?" "Does it matter to me that God did intervene?" "How important is the cross of Christ to me?" "Do I believe that *my* debt has been paid in full?" Our answers to these questions will tell us whether or not we are the prostitute or the Pharisee. It is not simply a matter of identifying with one or the other; it is a matter of *being* one or the other. It is not a matter of morbid introspection and being fixated on the worst expressions of our hearts, but of searching ourselves. Once I admit that I, at heart, am a murderer, a liar, an adulterer, a sexual deviant or addict, a slanderer or gossip, a thief, a drunkard, an idolater, filled with greed, etc., even if I am steeped in self-justifying, pharisaical self-righteousness, then and only then will I understand the wonder of the gospel: "Christ died for *my* sins!" Oh, the thought of it! "Am I captured by his love and gripped by his grace?" "Am I stirred by the cross?" "Do I love God?" "What do I understand about sin and grace?" "How do I respond to God's grace, on my behalf, at the cross?" "Does the blood of Jesus cause me to sorrow over my sins?" Loving God flows from understanding the gospel of grace. Personal devotion is rooted in the essence of the gospel. If I am going to be able to love God, I must be a gospel-driven follower of Christ. What is a definition of the gospel-driven Christian? Simply this: "The gospel-driven believer is a passionate recipient of God's revealed grace, one who is gripped by the greatness of that grace and now living for Christ and giving him everything, out of the depth of a heart filled with gratitude."

QUESTIONS FOR REFLECTION

1. How does *not* understanding our sinfulness prevent us from appreciating the gospel message?

2. What prevents us from being honest with ourselves about our sins?

3. What prevents us from being honest with others about our own sins?

4. With whom do you most identify—the prostitute or the Pharisee? Why did you choose one or the other, or both?

5. What is your story of personal brokenness due to your sin(s) and how does this story help you understand the gospel for yourself or explain it to others?

6. In what ways does understanding the good news of the cross give us peace?

ACTION POINTS

1. Write a poem, song, or a journal-type entry about a time you have been broken before the Lord and how the realization of the gospel healed your brokenness.

2. Consider sharing something of your story of brokenness and recovery through the gospel with another person who might benefit from hearing it.

PRAYER

"O Lord, may I always remember the words of the Apostle Paul, who understood your grace: 'But by the grace of God I am what I am, and his grace toward me was not in vain. On the contrary, I worked harder than any of them, though it was not I, but the grace of God that is with me' (1 Cor 15:10). May I be eager to search my heart and confess the ugliness I see within me. Help me to recognize my proclivity toward being a self-righteous Pharisee, denying my sin and lacking in my love to you. May my vision of what the cross cost Jesus spurn me unto greater love and service to you. Amen."

Chapter 8

Passionate People of Scripture

If you have not chosen the Kingdom of God first,
it will in the end make no difference what you have chosen instead.

WILLIAM LAW

God never measures the mind. . . .
He always puts His tape measure in the heart.

CORRIE TEN BOOM

Press forward. Do not stop, do not linger in your journey,
but strive for the mark set before you.

GEORGE WHITEFIELD

UNCONTAINABLE PASSION

I never met Mrs. Pace and, to this day, I regret that I passed on multiple opportunities to personally encounter her face to face. In my mind, all that I retain are images of what she looked like as my mother would describe her circumstances to me. Even as I write, I am kicking myself for not going to visit this elderly lady just once in my childhood. Mrs. Pace was a member of the church I grew up in as a boy but I never knew her to attend the church. I'm sure that she did at one time, and probably for many years, but to my knowledge she was never there when I was there (which was often).

Beginning in my early teenage years, my mother would go to visit Mrs. Pace at a nursing home located in upstate South Carolina, probably about an hour from my hometown of Greenville. Often, being a kid marooned at home for the summer or during a weekend, my mother would invite me to join her for one of these trips to visit this "shut in" woman. Of course, what teenage boy would go with his mother on a two-hour round-trip journey to visit an elderly woman in a nursing home? No matter how bored I might be, I wasn't up for the trip. Yes, I still regret it.

What did I miss? Well, the stories are consistent. My mother would *always* return and essentially say the same thing: "I went to visit Mrs. Pace to bless her in her loneliness and suffering, but instead, I was greatly blessed!" I heard our pastor, among other members of our church, say the same thing. And I could only envision what they experienced. You see, as I recall the narrative, Mrs. Pace became afflicted with a severe case of rheumatoid arthritis around the age of fifty. Her condition became so serious that eventually she had to move into a nursing home where she lived under constant care. Her body had shrunk up in such a deformed manner that she was balled up into about a three-foot figure. Her bed was a large children's crib into which she easily fit. She lay there constantly, taken care of by the nursing home staff. I believe that they would move her outside at times when the weather was nice. Otherwise, her life was as sedentary and immobile (and probably painful, although I never heard that expressed) as could possibly be.

As I recall, she was in her seventies during my teenage years. But the stories of those who visited her were all very similar. When they went into her room, she was radiant. She loved having visitors. She would talk incessantly to them but would never complain. Instead, she would talk about the Lord. She would quote many scriptures by heart to those who were usually looking down on her in her crib. And most stirring, I believe, is that she would burst into praise by singing many familiar hymns memorized from her years attending the local church! She would sing in joy while the visitors would watch and listen in amazement. Honestly, these stories were difficult to imagine, except that those who visited her, including my mom, rehearsed them over and over again in my hearing.

Mrs. Pace was a woman who knew God. She loved his church and had been faithful to it in her earlier years. She knew the Word of God and could quote it with significant meaning and application to life as she knew and experienced it. She most certainly had passion, as evidenced by her ability to burst out into joyful songs about her Lord and Savior upon being visited. Surely, this was a sight to be seen. Why the Lord leaves such testimonies of his grace in obscure places is a mystery to me (interestingly, the Apostle Paul actually spent much of his ministry life in prison). Mrs. Pace's behavior was based upon the truth of God's Word and her emotions reflected the inspiration that the Holy Spirit gave her. Her actions spoke louder than words, but in this case her actions were her words—memorized Scripture and song. She was passionate about her God and her passion could not be contained, even in a broken body or by the confinement of a crib in a nursing home—for years!

In this chapter, I simply want to list and briefly reflect upon some biblical passages that describe a few of the passionate people of the Scriptures. In these passages, we see followers of Christ and lovers of God expressing their emotions and heartfelt desires as these flow out of lives transformed by grace.

THE APOSTLE PAUL—PULSATING PASSION

The Apostle Paul is a man teeming with passion and there is no shortage of Scripture passages exhibiting that passion. I want us simply to look at a few of them.

1. 1 Corinthians 15:9–10—*God's Grace*:

> Last of all, as to one untimely born, he appeared also to me. For I am the least of the apostles, unworthy to be called an apostle, because I persecuted the church

of God. But by the grace of God I am what I am, and his grace toward me was not in vain. On the contrary, I worked harder than any of them, though it was not I, but the grace of God that is with me.

If anyone understands the grace of God, it is the Apostle Paul. Earlier in this passage, he recounts how Christ revealed himself to Paul. What a wonder, since he is so undeserving. Gifted, energetic, and a Type A personality, Paul is completely on the wrong track and fighting against the work of God, even persecuting the body of Christ. Paul discovers how misdirected his efforts are and how God has condescended to him, revealing himself in powerful fashion on the Damascus Road. He has been called to serve and suffer for Christ. Forgiveness for sins so large—this is the grace of God! What is Paul's response to God's grace? Passion! He labors for God with all of his might. Yet, ultimately, Paul's passion is a result of God's grace in his life. He cannot *not* respond. Christ gave his all for Paul the sinner, and Paul, in return, gives his all for Christ, but only through the strength that God has given him!

2. Philippians 3:7–11—*Knowing Christ*:

But whatever gain I had, I counted as loss for the sake of Christ. Indeed, I count everything as loss because of the surpassing worth of knowing Christ Jesus my Lord. For his sake I have suffered the loss of all things and count them as rubbish, in order that I may gain Christ and be found in him, not having a righteousness of my own that comes from the law, but that which comes through faith in Christ, the righteousness from God that depends on faith—that I may know him and the power of his resurrection, and may share his sufferings, becoming like him in his death, that by any means possible I may attain the resurrection from the dead.

In this passage, the Apostle Paul has just summarized a catalog of his personal accomplishments, attainments that he has realized have become totally worthless in light of the glory of Christ. Indeed, his personal resume is worth rubbish, trash, refuse to be tossed out, since none of it leads him to Christ and knowing him. All he wants is Christ's righteousness, trusting in the only One who can keep and fulfill the very law that Paul has tried to obey but could not. He now so identifies with Christ—his person and his work—that he is willing to lose all things, not only to have Christ, but to share in Christ's sufferings and to live in the power of Christ's presence and strength. Paul's death means Christ's life! Paul's passion in this passage is overwhelming, humbling, and inspiring to any who read it with a desire to know Christ alone!

3. 2 Corinthians 5:13–15—*Crazy Passion:*

> For if we are beside ourselves, it is for God; if we are in our right mind, it is for you. For the love of Christ controls us, because we have concluded this: that one has died for all, therefore all have died; and he died for all, that those who live might no longer live for themselves but for him who for their sake died and was raised.

In the context of this passage, Paul writes with eternity fully in mind. He can see (and probably personally recognizes) the frailty and groaning of human flesh, the hope of life immortal, and the sobering judgment seat of Christ! His words are about to leap into an impassioned plea for reconciliation with God, knowing what it means to fear him. If Paul sounds crazy (or out of his mind) through the realization of these overwhelming realities, it is because he has become gripped by God and his unbelievable love. If he sounds sane, his sensible words are written to prepare the believers at Corinth for eternity. He is an ambassador for God, appealing "madly" for others to be reconciled with God while there is still time! *Now* is the time of favor! Why? "For our sake he made him to be sin who knew no sin, so that in him we might become the righteousness of God" (5:21). Paul's passion flows out of an understanding that Christ died for our sins and became sin for us, enduring its penalty on the cross. Conversely, Christ provides a righteousness for us that we cannot supply. The thought of this twofold provision, in light of eternal judgment, is too great to contain within. Paul's passion bleeds all over the page as it pulsates from his pen!

4. Acts 20:18–19; 31; 36–38—*Weeping Hearts:*

> You yourselves know how I lived among you the whole time from the first day that I set foot in Asia, serving the Lord with all humility and with tears and with trials that happened to me through the plots of the Jews. . . . Therefore be alert, remembering that for three years I did not cease night or day to admonish every one with tears. . . . And when he had said these things, he knelt down and prayed with them all. And there was much weeping on the part of all; they embraced Paul and kissed him, being sorrowful most of all because of the word he had spoken, that they would not see his face again. And they accompanied him to the ship.

There is an old saying that you never want to see a grown man cry. I believe it is based on the thought that if a grown man is crying, the crisis must be a great one. Weeping demonstrates deep feelings and multiple weepers combine to portray immeasurable sorrow. Paul's passion includes tears, and apparently lots of them. Tears can sometimes be contagious, but it appears from this passage that the tears among these grown men flow from a mutual love for one another. Paul explains that his intense and long-term ministry has been punctuated with tears. What a testimony to be seen by those who want to be passionate people for Christ. Paul's ministry among the believers at Ephesus has contained hardships that fostered tears. For three years, he has tearfully taught and loved them (admonition involves powerful, honest love), and as they part, probably never to see one another again on this earth, the tears overflow, as do hugs and kisses. Christian brotherhood—grown men weeping. Passion flowing and falling, all over the ground!

5. Romans 9:1–3; 10:1—*Unceasing Anguish:*

> I am speaking the truth in Christ—I am not lying; my conscience bears me witness in the Holy Spirit—that I have great sorrow and unceasing anguish in my heart. For I could wish that I myself were accursed and cut off from Christ for the sake of my brothers, my kinsmen

according to the flesh. . . . Brothers, my heart's desire and prayer to God for them is that they may be saved.

These are some of the most sobering words that the Apostle Paul ever utters. He is willing to sacrifice not only his own life, but his very soul for the people of his beloved nation of Israel. He recognizes their spiritual blindness and lostness, and the eternal judgment that they are to incur due to their rejection of Christ. He is consumed by the consequential judgment of God upon their contempt for his gracious plan. Paul's heart is broken because they have rejected God's plan of salvation. His passion for their recovery involves great sorrow and constant anguish of heart, such that he would be willing to lose or forfeit his soul for their salvation.

HANNAH—IMPASSIONED BY GOD'S PROVISION

1 Samuel 2:1–3:

> And Hannah prayed and said, "My heart exults in the Lord; my horn is exalted in the Lord. My mouth derides my enemies, because I rejoice in your salvation. There is none holy like the Lord: for there is none besides you; there is no rock like our God. Talk no more so very proudly, let not arrogance come from your mouth; for the Lord is a God of knowledge, and by him actions are weighed."

Hannah is a grieving, childless woman who, though troubled by her inability to have a child (while her husband, Elkanah's, second wife was easily bearing children), understands that "the dark days of the judges" exist because God's people have lacked a man to lead them. Her prayer in 1 Samuel 2 is based upon the present need of a godless nation. If only the Lord will give her a son, she will give the boy back to the Lord to lead God's people. She is "all in" with God's plan, enough that she will *donate* her son to the Lord! If the Lord blesses her womb, the blessing will be returned to him. He does bless her, and she keeps her word. In our passionate passage above, we see a woman overcome by the greatness of God.

Only he is holy—all people must humble themselves before him. He works; he answers prayer; he meets the deepest need of our hearts and our pain; he provides for us and his people. Even in your struggles, seek the Lord and, as he answers, let your passion result in exultant joy focusing on him!

THE APOSTLE PETER—PASSIONATE FAITH

1. John 6:66–69:

> After this many of his disciples turned back and no lon-
> ger walked with him. So Jesus said to the Twelve, "Do
> you want to go away as well?" Simon Peter answered
> him, "Lord, to whom shall we go? You have the words
> of eternal life, and we have believed, and have come to
> know, that you are the Holy One of God."

Jesus has just confounded the crowds, the multitude who had been following him seemingly for all the wrong reasons. He perplexes them by declaring that they must eat his flesh and drink his blood. He declares that he is the bread of life—the manna that comes down from heaven. If they feed on the bread he offers, un-like the wilderness wanderers of Moses' time, they will live forever. Many of those listening begin to grumble, questioning the sensi-bility of such teaching. Jesus explains that only the Spirit gives life; otherwise, they will not believe. No one can come to him unless it is granted by the Father. The teaching is too heavy and mysterious for many of those listening and they walk away. So, Jesus turns to his disciples and confronts them with the question that plagues all believers at sometime in their walk with Christ: Do we want to follow this man of mystery? And, can we believe him when we don't understand? With a deep-seated passion of faith, Peter, who so often flies off the handle in his emotions, provides the very set-tling answer that has soothed the bothersome thoughts of so many believers over the centuries: There is nowhere else to turn. You are the only One with words of eternal life—we believe! Indeed, we know that you are the Holy One of God. Our passion remains even if our understanding is limited.

2. 1 Peter 1:8–9

> Though you have not seen him, you love him. Though you do not now see him, you believe in him and rejoice with joy that is inexpressible and filled with glory, obtaining the outcome of your faith, the salvation of your souls.

After his failure (triple denial of Christ prior to his crucifixion) and restoration by the resurrected Jesus, Peter becomes a shepherd to the fledgling church of the first century. He does so by writing letters to those believers, Jew and Gentile, scattered abroad throughout the region north and west of Jerusalem (now known as Turkey). His first letter addresses their obvious suffering on behalf of their belief in Christ. In this correspondence, inspired by the Holy Spirit, Peter expertly applies God's grace to these Christ-followers' tribulation. He encourages them to look by faith—as their faith is tested—toward the coming revelation of Jesus. His next words—our text above—are so full of heartfelt passion and faith in the reality of Christ that the reader (or listener) can almost feel the power of joy inexpressible and of glory soon to be revealed. Peter believes! Even though we cannot see Christ, the reality of his resurrection, his ascension, and his coming revelation thrill the soul beyond measure. The emotions are inexplicable! If the reader is not gripped by similar expressions of "soul" exhilaration, he may not know the Jesus of whom Peter speaks!

ESTHER—PROVIDENTIAL PASSION

Esther 4:12–17:

> And they told Mordecai what Esther had said. Then Mordecai told them to reply to Esther, "Do not think to yourself that in the king's palace you will escape any more than all the other Jews. For if you keep silent at this time, relief and deliverance will rise for the Jews from another place, but you and your father's house will

perish. And who knows whether you have not come to the kingdom for such a time as this?" Then Esther told them to reply to Mordecai, "Go, gather all the Jews to be found in Susa, and hold a fast on my behalf, and do not eat or drink for three days, night or day. I and my young women will also fast as you do. Then I will go to the king, though it is against the law, and if I perish, I perish." Mordecai then went away and did everything as Esther had ordered him.

In the book of Esther, we find a young Hebrew woman who is placed in a position of great influence when she becomes the Queen of Persia through quite a few unlikely circumstances. All of these circumstances are works of a God who is never explicitly mentioned in the book itself. Due to their disobedience, the nation of Israel has been removed from their homeland, disciplined by God, and dispersed into slavery. As he has disciplined them, he has refrained from actively working among his people. They have become known, throughout the book, by an unbecoming name— Jews—and have found themselves threatened with eradication due to some despicable devising by one resentful subject of the king, a man named Haman.

However, Esther's uncle, Mordecai, recognizes that the unspoken hand of the God of Israel has placed her in a position to potentially save the lives of her people. Esther discerns that she certainly has arisen to a strategic position, as Mordecai says, "for such a time as this." With both this providential position and time in mind, she will approach the king, at the risk of her life. Understanding the providence of God, her passion to give up her life for the sake of her own is evident. She is fully engaged in the needs of God's kingdom. In the large scheme of things, we realize that God's redemptive channel for the world, the nation of Israel, is being jeopardized. But, they survive and will be used strategically in a future day, as a means to gospel proclamation. The synagogues they will build in a foreign land will provide open doors for the Apostle Paul to proclaim his message. All of this is due to the providential passion of a young woman who is willing to give her all to the living God, though he seems absent at the time.

DAVID—PASSION ON HIS SLEEVE

1. 1 Samuel 24:1–7:

> When Saul returned from following the Philistines, he was told, "Behold, David is in the wilderness of Engedi." Then Saul took three thousand chosen men out of all Israel and went to seek David and his men in front of the Wildgoats' Rocks. And he came to the sheepfolds by the way, where there was a cave, and Saul went in to relieve himself. Now David and his men were sitting in the innermost parts of the cave. And the men of David said to him, "Here is the day of which the Lord said to you, 'Behold, I will give your enemy into your hand, and you shall do to him as it shall seem good to you.'" Then David arose and stealthily cut off a corner of Saul's robe. And afterward David's heart struck him, because he had cut off a corner of Saul's robe. He said to his men, "The Lord forbid that I should do this thing to my lord, the Lord's anointed, to put out my hand against him, seeing he is the Lord's anointed." So David persuaded his men with these words and did not permit them to attack Saul. And Saul rose up and left the cave and went on his way.

There are so many passages, particularly in the psalms that he wrote, that exhibit the passion of the shepherd boy David, who eventually becomes king of Israel. In this passage, written about Saul's pursuit of David prior to his becoming king, we see one reason why David is called "a man after God's own heart" (1 Sam 13:14; Acts 13:22). David has the opportunity to kill Saul, and although all he does is deftly cut off a corner of Saul's robe, his conscience (or heart) bothers him so deeply that he regrets his decision and permits Saul to escape his grasp. David proves his character, and these actions in regard to Saul are based upon David's desire to please and honor the Lord—certainly an attitude that engenders passion.

2. Psalm 42:1–2:

> As a deer pants for flowing streams, so pants my soul for
> you, O God. My soul thirsts for God, for the living God.
> When shall I come and appear before God?

Although David's name is not mentioned in this psalm, many scholars believe it is written by his hand, most probably when he was on the run from his rebellious son, Absalom. The psalmist fondly remembers what it meant to both worship God and to join the procession of God's people in worship in the holy city of Jerusalem. His passion for God is vigorously displayed in the midst of his loss of worship—quite the needed testimony to our present day, in which worship of God, particularly corporate worship, is treated so cavalierly. Miss worship and neglect the church? No problem! And the actual problem among those who say they are God's people is that there is no consuming, heartfelt passion for the living God! Later in the psalm, as well as in its extension, Psalm 43—we see that David battles depression over both his plight and his loss of hope in God. He is in mourning and "cast down." Can passion cause depression? Loss of God and deprivation of worship in the midst of great trial can cause a person to question all of life. The answer for David is the altar (43:4), God's holy hill and his dwelling place. Worship among God's people is the answer for a downcast heart. May we have a passion for worshipping God in the assembly of his people!

3. Psalm 51:10–13:

> Create in me a clean heart, O God, and renew a right
> spirit within me. Cast me not away from your presence,
> and take not your Holy Spirit from me. Restore to me the
> joy of your salvation, and uphold me with a willing spirit.
> Then I will teach transgressors your ways, and sinners
> will return to you.

Sometimes David appears to be an enigma, a contradiction in terms. He is "a man after God's own heart," yet he also fails God in a great way. In 2 Samuel 11, we see David guilty of the neglect of kingly duties (leading in war), lust, adultery, deceit and conspiracy, oppression of the poor, murder, war crimes, and false spirituality. Added to the list is an apparent unwillingness to confess or uncover his sin, and probably the smug and reassuring sense that he has gotten away with it all. In the narrative, all of these actions are combined into one act, i.e., the sin of adultery with Bathsheba. This "thing" displeases the Lord! Eventually, David will undergo a most thorough and sharp rebuke by the prophet Nathan, as described in 1 Samuel 12. And then he writes this psalm. It is dripping with passion, a passion to be restored to the God he has disobeyed and ignored. How deeply he desires God's Spirit to work in him and uphold him. How desperately he pleads for the joy in the Lord he has previously known. If God will forgive him and restore his joy, he will passionately teach other sinners about God's grace and they will, like him, repent. God's grace overflows into evangelistic passion from those who experience it!

ASAPH—POINTED POETIC PASSION

1. Psalm 73:23–26:

   Nevertheless, I am continually with you; you hold my right hand. You guide me with your counsel, and afterward you will receive me to glory. Whom have I in heaven but you? And there is nothing on earth that I desire besides you. My flesh and my heart may fail, but God is the strength of my heart and my portion forever.

2. Psalm 77:12–15:

   I will ponder all your work, and meditate on your mighty deeds. Your way, O God, is holy. What god is great like our God? You are the God who works wonders; you have made known your might among the peoples. You with your arm redeemed your people, the children of Jacob and Joseph.

Asaph is known as a poet and a singer who wrote a number of the psalms. Psalms 50 and 73–83 are attributed to him. Asaph wrestles with the injustice and evil in the world and the fact that God's people are so often persecuted, while those who seek their own way ironically succeed and prevail. However, Asaph realizes that God's enemies will not ultimately succeed! Asaph's passion and poetic writings are pointed toward the hope that God will eventually intervene and judge his enemies. His psalms are often imprecatory, calls for God to bring justice to his people as they suffer for his sake. Asaph's passion is expressed in the confidence that, despite God's seeming absence at times in the life of the believer, God is indeed with us, will guide us to glory, and is all we need on earth for strength and spiritual sustenance. Psalm 73 is my favorite psalm because, although Asaph appears to sink low in faith, he ultimately resolves all his questions of doubt by looking at the bottom line of God's judgment. And he finds the assurance of God's presence, work, and judgment for his wavering soul! Passion for God prevails!

HABAKKUK—STEADY PASSION

1. Habakkuk 2:4:

   Behold, his soul is puffed up; it is not upright within him, but the righteous shall live by his faith.

2. Habakkuk 2:20:

   But the LORD is in his holy temple; let all the earth keep silence before him.

3. Habakkuk 3:17–19:

   Though the fig tree should not blossom, nor fruit be on the vines, the produce of the olive fail and the fields yield no food, the flock be cut off from the fold and there be no herd in the stalls, yet I will rejoice in the LORD; I will take joy in the God of my salvation. GOD, the LORD, is my strength; he makes my feet like the deer's; he makes me tread on my high places.

The book of Habakkuk is written at a time when the nation of Judah is reveling in ungodliness. They are far from Jehovah, but Habakkuk cannot understand why God does not judge his people. The Lord reveals to Habakkuk that he will send the Babylonians (or the Chaldeans), a very evil nation from the north, to punish his people. Habakkuk is incredulous about God's plan—that he will use greater evil to judge Israel's evil—but he also realizes that it must be accepted, as "the righteous shall live by his faith." The reason we can walk by faith is because a holy God, who will do no wrong, rules over all things. We must hush our questions before his awesome presence. Ultimately, this steady passion of Habakkuk is demonstrated by his willingness to lose everything and to find his joy in the Lord, who provides salvation for his people. Believers can move forward with a passionate resolve because the Lord strengthens them even in the greatest of trials.

OTHER PASSIONATE PEOPLE OF SCRIPTURE

The list I have compiled is quite incomplete. There are other people who leap off the page in the Scriptures who demonstrate or exemplify great passion for the Lord. Some of them are: Joseph (Genesis 39—Passion for Purity); Moses (Exodus 32:30–34; 33:12–23—Passionate Intercession); Daniel (Daniel 9—Passionate Prayer); Nehemiah (Nehemiah 13—Passionate Leadership); and Stephen (Acts 6:1–6; 7:51–60—Passionate Service and Preaching). We would do well to also study their lives and passion as we attempt to answer the question, "Do I Love God?"

QUESTIONS FOR REFLECTION

1. Which of the "passionate people of Scripture" above are most moving to your soul? Why?

2. What are the circumstances or situations that spawn passion for God in your heart?

3. Who is the most passionate person for Christ that you know and how is that passion expressed?

4. To what might we attribute a loss of passion for the Lord and a failure to live out the Christian life?

5. How do trials and difficulties either test or prove our passion for the Lord?

ACTION POINTS

1. Using one or more of the passages above, or simply in your own words, write out a passionate prayer to the Lord from your heart and post it somewhere as a reminder of your desire to love and serve him.

2. Find the hymn "When I Survey the Wondrous Cross" and sing it with a joyful heart as a prayer unto the Lord.

PRAYER

"O Lord, enter into the life of my soul and give me a greater passion to live for you, day by day, even moment by moment. I pray that you will not leave me alone, but will patiently humble me in such a way that I will realize that I am fully dependent upon you. I give you myself and desire to fully give you my all. Help me to deny myself, take up my cross daily, and follow you. May my heart sing with joyful contemplation, 'Were this whole realm of nature mine, that were a present far too small. Love so amazing, so divine, demands my soul, my life, my all.' I pray this prayer in the blessed name of Christ. Amen."

Chapter 9

Developing a Life of Devotion

Prayer is not monologue, but dialogue; God's voice is its most essential part. Listening to God's voice is the secret of the assurance that He will listen to mine.

ANDREW MURRAY

We must seek, in studying God, to be led to God.

J. I. PACKER

Thou art coming to a King, large petitions with thee bring, for His grace and power are such none can ever ask too much.

JOHN NEWTON

DEVOTED LOVE

"Do I love God?" Love is devotion to another. "Am I devoted to God?" Devotion to God involves all of life—the mind, the emotions, and the will—daily yielding yourself to the lordship of Christ in every endeavor. It means loving the Lord will all of your heart, mind, soul, and strength. It means denying yourself and living constantly in his presence. Of course, giving yourself totally and wholly to the Lord every moment of your life is impossible since we are sinners at heart and finite in strength, resolve, and ability. Nevertheless, God's people are called to follow Christ (Matt 4:19) and to seek God and his kingdom first (Matt 6:33), to pursue righteousness and godliness (1 Tim 6:11), to know Christ (Phil 3:8, 10), and to press on toward the goal for the prize of the upward call of God in Christ Jesus (Phil 3:14). If we are to pursue such wholehearted devotion to the Lord, we recognize that much effort is required. Understanding the gospel of grace naturally prompts a grateful pursuit of the God of grace.

If we are to gratefully pursue God wholly, then I believe that we must spend time with him. If we are going to spend our eternity with him, we must begin now. We have been redeemed into a relationship with God, as amazing as that sounds. Jesus said, "And this is eternal life, that they know you the only true God, and Jesus Christ whom you have sent" (John 17:3). Knowing God—that is life and that is why we exist! We have seen previously that what is most important in life is understanding *who* God is and knowing him in intimate relationship, a personal relationship that comes about by faith in Christ, God's Son. The probing question is, "Will we pursue this relationship?"

So, I have a question: "Can you love God without spending special and intimate time with him?" Furthermore, "Can you love anyone with your whole being without spending time with and getting to know him/her better?" If you are married, "Can you love your spouse without spending special and intimate time with her/ him?" Time, effort, expression, honesty, and transparency in communication are the keys to building a solid, lasting relationship with another person. If the Christian life is a walk with God, then a life of prayer is a vital dimension of that walk. Prayer involves both speaking to God and listening to God. Listening requires reading his Word. Without his Word, we do not know how to pray properly. In this chapter, I wish to address some practical ways for a believer in Christ to spend time with God.

There are many excellent books written about prayer,[1] so I am not going to do an exhaustive treatment of the biblical teaching on the subject of prayer. However, I do want to address the necessity and priority of developing a personal devotional life. World renowned evangelist and leader Dr. Billy Graham was heavily influenced by his wife's, the late Ruth Graham, father and missionary physician to China, Dr. Nelson Bell. Dr. Graham, observing the strong leadership of Dr. Bell and the way in which God used his father-in-law, once wrote, "It took me some time to realize that this tremendous strength came from his private devotional life. He has never been ostentatious about it. It is a lifetime habit that he takes for granted."[2]

I hope that this chapter might assist you, in some way, to deepen your prayer life. My primary purpose will be to give you some ideas about carrying forth a regular or daily prayer life, with the underlying purpose of growing closer to and more deeply in love with the living God and his Son, Jesus Christ. May you develop a lifetime habit that you take for granted each and every day!

Let us now consider what it means to have a devotional strategy. A devotional strategy is designed to help us figure out the why, what, when, where, and how of developing and spending consistent time with God.

WHY?

Briefly, we will discuss the purposes for having a regularly scheduled devotional life.

1. First of all, as has been mentioned above, we want to know God. The Puritans saw the Christian life as "friendship with God." Our life is a walk of faith with the living God. When you consider it, the Christian life should be lived moment by moment and as a daily relationship. Special time set aside with God will only enhance the growth of the relationship.

1. Listed at the end of this chapter.
2. Quoted in Pollock, *Foreign Devil in China*, 67.

2. We grow in greater love for God and we spend time worshipping him. Worship is a purpose for which we have been created. Private or personal worship is a vital element of the devotional life and complements our public worship in the local church.

3. Using the Scriptures, we hear God's will and learn what he desires of us. We also give our day to God—we hand it over to him and entrust ourselves to him.

4. A devotional life becomes a place of change in our lives. We pray, "God, come! Lord, meet me here and work in my heart, life, and circumstances." If we plead for him to come, he will!

5. If we pursue God devotionally, we will find a greater motivation for living the Christian life and we will also discover Holy Spirit–inspired encouragement for whatever we face each day.

The Puritans described morning and evening devotions with the terms "preview" and "review." Preview was their morning Scripture reading and prayer time, designed to focus upon the new and coming day. Preview prepared them to walk with God throughout the activities of the day. Review was their opportunity to pause at the end of the day and pray about their sins, failures, and disappointments, while recognizing God's faithfulness to them and giving thanks for his presence and grace throughout the day.

WHAT?

As we consider what is involved in having and maintaining our own personal devotion time, we must focus upon the Christian disciplines of prayer, Scripture reading, and meditation. A devotional life, or what many call a "quiet time," is actually a very simple pursuit. A basic order or structure would consist of the following:

1. Prayer (including praise and adoration)

2. Reading the Bible (and possibly other devotional material)

3. Meditation (reflecting upon what you have read)

4. Concluding with prayer (praying about what you have read and learned, confessing sin, and requesting grace for obedience and resolve)

5. Meditating upon the truths that you learned throughout the day or the next day

We will discuss the "how," or method of carrying forth the reading and meditation of a devotional life, in the section below.

As for the "what" of prayer, Martin Luther, known as the father of the Protestant Reformation, provided a very simple acrostic for his congregation, one that is used very frequently today. I find it to be an excellent guide for organizing your time in personal prayer and devotion, as it covers the necessary elements of a prayer life. The acrostic is ACTS:

1. Adoration: Spend time praising and worshiping God. We begin here, first, because God is deserving of our praise and, secondly, because words of adoration move us away from our natural inclination, that of praying for ourselves (supplication).

2. Confession: Prayer must be transparent and open, so we must learn to honestly tell our sins to God. It should be only natural to confess our sins and moral failings if we have just spent time focusing on the greatness and holiness of our awesome God. Some have even suggested that the acrostic should be CATS because we should always begin by examining ourselves, being certain not to come to God harboring unconfessed sin in our hearts. Of course, the acrostic is only a formula or suggested guideline, and the praying believer can start anywhere as long as her heart is genuine before the Lord.

3. Thanksgiving: We continue with thanks because we recognize that, through Christ, a holy God has forgiven the sins we have just confessed. And, of course, we could spend endless time thanking God for the blessings he has sent our way since

there are so many. Gratitude is a constant attitude when it comes to prayer.

4. Supplication: Lastly, since this is our most natural form of prayer, we ask. Asking and petitioning are certainly appropriate because the Lord's brother James reminds us that we have not because we ask not (Jas 4:2). In the Sermon on the Mount, Jesus states, "Ask, and it will be given to you; seek, and you will find; knock, and it will be opened to you" (Matt 7:7). One of the primary Greek words for prayer is *deomai*. *Deomai* is actually the word that signifies "to petition" or "to beg," so by this word alone we are made to understand that we come to God with our needs as beggars. The word also implies that those needs are urgent requests. Our Father is glad to hear all of our needs and begging! Finally, I should mention that I have heard that the acrostic SCAT is the one we should avoid because it places our supplication *first*. I do prefer ACTS and CATS over SCAT (TACS works too), but I do not believe that there is a mandatory acrostic to follow. Basically, we should simply seek the Lord and develop all four attitudes in our prayers as a matter of posture and practice.

Lastly, I must mention that a part of one's devotional life should be meditation. Christian meditation is simply the process of dwelling on the thoughts or truths that you have just read, with a hope that the truths will take hold in your heart and life. The word for "meditate" in the Old Testament (cf. Josh 1:8; Ps 1:2) means to muse, to speak (as if to yourself), and to utter (with repetitive thought). The believer is wise to let the words that she has read sink into her heart and this is best done by taking time to pause and consider them during her personal devotions. Then, she can keep the concept on her mind (finding its meaning) throughout the day, "musing" on it over and over again for its intended effect in her life (discovering its application). The Navigators ministry that I mentioned earlier taught me about "The Navigator Hand." This concept teaches that we learn from God's Word in various ways. The four fingers are 1) hearing, 2) reading, 3) studying, and

4) memorizing. But the primary point of the illustration is that the only way to fully *grasp* the Word of God is by holding on to it with the thumb. And the thumb in the illustration is 5) meditation. We gain a grasp of the Word through musing over it. We lose the grasp when we fail to meditate on its meaning and application. So, part of the "what" of one's devotional life should be Christian meditation. With meditation in mind, possibly, our acrostic should be ACTSM!

WHEN?

Here, we consider the ever-pressing question, and one that often elicits a lot of guilt in the life of the Christian: What *time* of day should a believer choose to spend time with God? Jesus obviously spent early morning hours in places of solitude, as seen in Mark 1:35, "And rising very early in the morning, while it was still dark, he departed and went out to a desolate place, and there he prayed." Elsewhere, however, see also Luke 6:12, "In these days he went out to the mountain to pray, and all night he continued in prayer to God." Jesus prayed early in the morning, but sometimes at night and through the night. I personally believe that the place, or the selection of a location determined by access to solitude, is more important than the time of day.

Morning, prior to all of the busy distractions that occur throughout an action-packed day of responsibility, would be an obvious choice for meeting God and preparing for the remainder of the day. I might add that my mother, who became a Christian a couple of years after marrying my father, realized that once she began to have and raise children, the only quiet time of her day would be before everyone in the household awoke. So, for approximately fifty years, she had her daily devotions from 4:30 a.m. until around 6:15 a.m. I have *not* followed her example! As another personal example, my wife, Cathy, now an empty nester, often uses the breakfast time to read the Scriptures and pray. I know people who have their devotions—at least their prayer time—in the car, while driving to work and/or sitting in traffic on the way to work.

That location isn't ideal and is certainly not without distraction, but I am pleased that they are trying!

Evening, particularly before bedtime, can be—for night people like myself—a great time to review the day, consider our victories, sins, failures, and blessings, and to meet with God in praise, gratitude, confession, and fellowship. If you use night time for devotions and are constantly falling asleep while you read Scripture or pray, evening probably isn't your time. Afternoon would be an unusual time for a habit of prayer, since afternoons are not very quiet or calm. Maybe an afternoon time would work for someone (I've known professionals who take fifteen-minute power naps in the afternoon in order to get through the rest of the day—why not fifteen-minute *power prayers* in the middle of the day?), but generally the afternoon doesn't seem very conducive to privacy, solitude, less distraction, or calm. Possibly a special time on Sunday afternoon would work, if your Lord's Day is not focused on activity. But, as a regular time, afternoon would appear less desirable.

So, should it be morning, afternoon, or evening? All this being said, there is no reason not to use all three times or, like the Puritans' "preview" and "review," have some form of personal devotions in both the morning and the evening, as your schedule and habits allow. Seeking God's face is the key! I was once sitting in a presbytery meeting (a group of ministers and ruling elders meeting together from various churches in a region) and a candidate for the ministry was being examined for a transfer of membership. Thankfully, in addition to questioning the man about his theology and Bible understanding, the presbytery also inquired about the man's walk with God and his devotional life. I don't remember who he was or what church he was serving, but I do recall how he responded. He said, "My mother taught me to spend time each day with God. She said, 'It doesn't matter what time of the day you spend having private devotions with God—morning, afternoon, early evening, or late at night before bedtime. Just be sure to *give God the best time* of your day!'" I believe that she gave her son excellent advice and that is the advice I give to you. Give God the best time!

WHERE?

Sometimes finding the right place is the biggest challenge. As I mentioned above, I think solitude is more important than the time chosen for personal devotions. Again, if we look at the practice of Jesus, we observe that he would *withdraw*. Luke 5:16 says, "But he would withdraw to desolate places and pray." Further in his Gospel, Luke writes, "Now it happened that as he was praying alone, the disciples were with him. And he asked them, 'Who do the crowds say that I am?'" (9:18). One of the themes of Luke's Gospel is to present Christ in his humanity. Jesus was fully man. Another theme in Luke's Gospel is that of prayer. Jesus the man needed to find the time and place for private prayer with the Father.

Jesus himself tells his fledgling followers early in his ministry in the Sermon on the Mount,

> And when you pray, you must not be like the hypocrites.
> For they love to stand and pray in the synagogues and at
> the street corners, that they may be seen by others. Truly,
> I say to you, they have received their reward. 6 But when
> you pray, go into your room and shut the door and pray
> to your Father who is in secret. And your Father who
> sees in secret will reward you. (Matt 6:5–6)

Privacy with the Father is a priority. Of course, Jesus is condemning the Pharisees' public prayer showmanship, but the point still appears clear. Pray to the Father in secret—find a place and seek intimacy with him as a friend. And a prayer closet isn't a bad idea either, if you have one large enough to use!

Jesus also appears to have a special place for prayer, and it is there that he goes as he faces his arrest, unjust beatings, and the impending crucifixion. Again, Luke tells us,

> And he came out and went, as was his custom, to the
> Mount of Olives, and the disciples followed him. And
> when he came to the place, he said to them, "Pray that
> you may not enter into temptation." And he withdrew
> from them about a stone's throw, and knelt down and
> prayed, saying, "Father, if you are willing, remove this

cup from me. Nevertheless, not my will, but yours, be done." (Luke 22:39–42)

The Mount of Olives must have been a very special place to Jesus because he apparently went there often. Just outside and east of the gates of Jerusalem, he would walk past the Garden of Gethsemane, up the hill, and, we would assume, find a private spot among the olive trees or at the top of the hill. The journey was a little over a mile, so it would take some effort, but at the same time it was not too far away. From the Mount of Olives one can look down upon the city of Jerusalem, so we can imagine that Jesus often prayed from this special place for the beloved city, "the place" of sacrifice where he would eventually give up his life on our behalf.

The choice of a place for prayer and personal devotions is never easy. In my own experience, in an effort to "get away," I have attempted private devotions in a myriad of locations. At college: in my college dorm room or on the dorm room breezeway porch (much revival occurred there), in my personal automobile late at night, on the top of my dorm (the roof, a very secluded and safe area), and walking down the street to the old dilapidated Columbia railroad station (now a very nice restaurant). Other places: on my living room couch (after other family members have gone to bed), in my office (early in the morning), in my bedroom on the bed or on the floor (when my wife is already asleep), in my backyard in the hammock, and walking in the woods or the local park (depending upon the safety and park regulations). I'm sure there are other places one could find and use as well.

I think that the key principle is privacy or solitude, where the place prevents distraction or disturbance. Seclusion and quiet would be important factors. Not having your cell phone along with you (or at least having it on silent) would be a very important consideration as well. The special place of prayer is a location where no one can find you but the Lord!

HOW?

As mentioned above, the three basic elements of a devotional life would include, prayer, reading, and meditation. Prayer, of course, includes adoration, confession of sin, thanksgiving, supplication, and meditation. Reading, particularly reading the Bible, is often the biggest challenge. Interestingly, some surveys have concluded that many Americans have not even read an *entire* book in the past year! Nevertheless, if there is a book that one should make a priority to read at any time in life, it would certainly be the book of books, God's Word. Go for it!

Here are some suggestions to help any individual who wants to read the Bible devotionally. First of all, read short sections of material in whatever book you are reading. Focus on a paragraph or a narrative (long or short—most Bible stories are not too long). Consider reading short books of the Bible, particularly the New Testament letters, in one setting to get a feel for what it might be like to receive and hear this letter read as an early church believer. Then return to the letter and read it in sections or paragraphs. Many ministers, ministries, churches, and other people encourage believers to read the Bible through in one year. That aspiration is an admirable goal. However, I don't encourage anyone to do it as a goal for their devotional time. It is fine if they do so, but I think the "pressure" to read so much Scripture in one setting overcomes the need to read it slowly, thoughtfully, and with the purpose of taking time to meditate on what you have read. If you wish to set aside a separate time to read a lot of Scripture so that you can complete the entire Bible in one year, you will still benefit spiritually from the Word of God, but I believe that you will lose the benefits of meditation and letting the material that you read sink in. In my opinion, meditating on Scripture is a priority, and time in your personal devotions should be allotted to it.

Other questions about the method of devotional reading frequently surface. I have been asked about the concept of studying the Bible while you are reading it devotionally. I certainly think that there are times to dig a little deeper while you read for the purpose of spiritual nourishment. Of course, reading the notes in a study Bible can make unclear matters in the text much more understandable. I have read two or three books of the Bible devotionally with a Bible commentary at hand in order to look up difficult material. I have read Ecclesiastes and Zechariah in that manner, and when I became a new believer I immediately went to the local Christian bookstore to purchase a very simple Bible commentary that I could read along with my very first reading of Scripture in the Gospel of Matthew. No one told me to do that and no one probably would. I actually didn't complete the commentary but it was helpful in the early days of being a new Christian and reading the Bible seriously for the first time ever.

Although I don't consider this quite the same as studying the Bible, I do recommend making notes in your Bible while you read it devotionally. Underlining verses that impact you greatly and/or placing an asterisk or some arrows by an important concept or circling the number of a special verse could all be used. I often write down the date of a reading or include a note on the page in the Bible about an impression or thought that hit me during the reading. Along with the date and note, I might add why it is significant to me. A marked Bible is not a means whereby we show off our spirituality. But a marked Bible should demonstrate that we are experiencing an interactive walk with God, listening and responding to him, and finding great comfort and encouragement in his character, promises, admonitions, rebukes, and conviction of sin.

What about devotional helps such as books or structured devotional guides? Speaking of devotional books, I once heard a campus staff person say, "What God will bless as a complement, he will curse as a substitute." I think that may be an overstatement, but he was trying to emphasize that the focus of our devotions should be upon the direct reading of God's Word. Nevertheless, many devotional books, such as *Our Daily Bread*, *The Upper Room*, Charles Spurgeon's *Morning and Evening* and *Cheque Book of Faith*, and Oswald Chamber's *My Utmost for His Highest*, among many others, have been a great blessing to believers over the past hundred years. Obviously, these are not the Word of God, but they are based on God's Word and can be profitable to the reader.

I also would suggest reading, as a complement to the Scriptures, books by the Puritans (there is an unlimited supply of these), such as *Valley of Vision*, a collection of Puritan prayers by Arthur Bennett, *Precious Remedies Against Satan's Devices* by Thomas Brooks, or *The Bruised Reed* by Richard Sibbes. Then there are books about God that are always profitable (mentioned previously), such as *The Knowledge of the Holy* by A. W. Tozer, *Knowing God* by Dr. J. I. Packer, *The Attributes of God* by A. W. Pink, and the exhaustive volume *Existence and Attributes of God* by Puritan writer Stephen Charnock.

Reading thoughtful theology books often expands the mind and should lead us to the worship of God. Reading historic creeds and confessions of faith, such as the Nicene Creed, the Westminster Confession of Faith, or the Heidelberg Confession can be nice complements to Scripture reading as well, and should provide some theological understanding on a given biblical topic. As for including some theology in your devotions, C. S. Lewis once wrote,

> For my own part I tend to find the doctrinal books often more helpful in devotion than the devotional books, and I rather suspect that the same experience may await many others. I believe that many who find that "nothing happens" when they sit down, or kneel down, to a book of devotion, would find that the heart sings unbidden while they are working their way through a tough bit of theology with a pipe in their teeth and a pencil in their hand.[3]

I agree completely with Professor Lewis, except that I never use a pipe or a pencil!

A few other helpful observations might be noted about the implementation of a regular devotional life. I think it is more than appropriate to sing songs, hymns, praise music, or choruses during your devotional time as a means to uplift your heart in praise. I keep one or two hymnals nearby, just in case I desire to do some singing. Biblically based music can cause the heart to

3. Lewis, *God in the Dock*, 205.

soar in God's presence. Of course, a secluded or remote location would be ideal, whether you can sing well or not! And, while I've rarely done it, I think it is appropriate to turn on your smartphone or laptop and sing along with a music video or a hymn or other Christian song. I also believe, if you have such an inclination, that a devotional time is a good occasion to write your own hymn, song, or poem unto the Lord. I have never done that explicitly, but I have written down some thoughts derived from my devotional reading or inspired by my prayer and meditation that might resemble something poetic. Those recorded thoughts are a joy to return to at a later time.

And that thought brings me to the topic of journaling or keeping a record of your devotional readings, thoughts, prayers, and impressions. Although I have almost never journaled in my devotions, I can most certainly encourage the practice. What a blessing it can be to write down daily or weekly thoughts from your time with God. What has he said? What have you heard? How has he spoken or revealed himself to you? How should you respond? What resolve does your time with God create? Were there any special verses or applicable thoughts? All of these questions reflect the benefit of maintaining one's thoughts about God and Scripture. And, for what it is worth, I recently surveyed the faculty at RTS Charlotte, where I presently teach, and one third of the faculty members stated that they keep journals of their time with God. Journaling is a good practice and you have to decide if keeping a spiritual journal is a method that fits you.

Related to what you do with your time in your devotions is the length of time that you spend in them. If you are a novice, the Navigators (a ministry with a military beginning, as well as a collegiate and publishing ministry) many years ago produced a pamphlet called *Seven Minutes with God.*[4] It uses the ACTS acrostic and structures the time like this:

---

4. This pamphlet is available free online at http://www.navigators.org/ www_navigators_org/media/navigators/tools/Disciple/2012%20October/D-1012-7minutes.pdf.

1. Half a Minute: Preparing Your Heart (Pray for Openness to Hear the Lord)

2. Four Minutes: Listening to God (Scripture Reading)

3. Two and a Half Minutes: Talking to God (Prayer, Based on the ACTS Acrostic)

The basic premise, which I think is brilliant, is that anyone can start with just seven minutes set aside for God each day. And once you get started, soon you will easily develop a devotional habit. As a consequence, the time will quickly grow beyond seven minutes because you will not be able to settle for such a short time of blessing with the Lord. I once heard a seminary professor say that if a full-time businessman is making the effort to spend at least five minutes each day with the Lord, he is really accomplishing something. When I first heard those words my countenance dropped. How could this be? But over the years, I see a lot of truth in the statement. He is trying and he is seeking. Should a busy layperson's personal time with God be longer than five or seven minutes? I believe that it could and should be. But, along with that professor, I also want to commend the man (or woman) who is making any time with the Lord each and every day. He/she is seeking him, finding blessing, and most probably growing in Christlikeness, while walking with a renewed Godward perspective as he/she faces the day.

As for the amount of time to set aside for personal prayer and devotions, I think that, for some, spending thirty minutes for a devotional session is a noble goal. Others will find an hour of time per day, although that would be rare. The seriously prayerful might set aside an hour or more for a prayer and devotional getaway in a secluded area. Some set aside an entire weekend or week and include fasting. The Navigators campus ministry in which I was involved, as well as the seminary I attended for my Master of Divinity degree, Columbia International University, both encouraged or sponsored "half-days of prayer" or even what they called "days of prayer" (which were actually only a few hours long and included personal, small-group, and large-group corporate prayer). Prayer is work but, for some reading this book, eventually it will become almost a hobby or a growing passion that you relish and pursue.

FAILURE?

This brings me to my final thought and a common question for the Christian who takes having personal devotions or a quiet time seriously: What if I miss or fail to have a devotional time? The reality is that there will be a day or days that you will not have a time of personal devotion. You may forget, become rushed, be interrupted with a special responsibility or with hosting guests and company, become ill, or simply be too tired. I have experienced all of those scenarios. Since I usually have my "extended" devotional time at night, sometimes I face fatigue from a long day and I simply say, "Lord, I am really tired and I am going straight to bed." He doesn't mind. I think he says, "Good night!" to my soul. We don't want our devotional life to become a legalistic, ritualistic "performance," lacking joy and the blessing of the relationship. Some days, I don't spend a lot of time close to or in deep conversation with my wife, but I still love her and she loves me. We catch up later. God, our Father, is like that and he can wait for us. He wants our well-being. A quiet time is not an act of superstition, as if we are looking for blessing from God because we have said our prayers!

Finally, I should address those times that might seem like a failure in the pursuit of personal devotional time with God, but actually are not. Here are some of the common experiences of believers as they persevere in their devotional lives, some feeling like failures and others bringing great comfort:

1. Sometimes the devotional life is dry—God doesn't seem present or to be speaking to her. The Word seems lifeless and the believer's soul is lifeless. Times like these require the believer to be persistent until the joy of the Lord breaks through.

2. Sometimes the time is blessed and God seems very close and is. The heart is assured of God's presence and there is a sense of the nearness to God.

3. Sometimes there is a sense of ecstasy, incredible joy, and lots of emotion. The believer feels like he is taken out of this world and has entered the heavenly places. God is a spirit, but at these times his spirit almost seems within the grasp of the believer's soul. These times may be rare but they can be very real. There is no formula for an experience such as this, but it resembles the vibrant revivals of the Great Awakenings in America's past. It is a revival of the soul on the individual level, and the believer is so awed by the goodness of God that the only reaction is joy inexpressible and possibly love ineffable.

4. Sometimes God seems absent and distant and the believer must simply come to God's throne by faith, trusting that he hears and will answer. This experience could occur for a very short time or could be an example of what is classically known as "the dark night of the soul." The dark night of the soul is a period of such deep suffering and sometimes agony, such that one wonders if God exists at all.

5. Sometimes the believer doesn't want to spend any time with God, but disciplines himself to almost "go through the motions." Surprisingly, walking through the discipline of prayer, Scripture reading, and/or meditation becomes a very blessed time and the believer is so very grateful that he pursued God despite his original disinterest or unwillingness.

6. Sometimes the believer just loves to have her personal devotions and really looks forward to it every night. She is disappointed if, for some reason, she misses the time with God.

7. Sometimes, as mentioned above, the believer is simply exhausted from a busy day and simply goes to bed tired, or is weary from a previous short or poor night's sleep and needs to skip the discipline. God is still in his presence and will watch over him as he faces the new day.

No matter what might be the result of your devotional time with the Lord, hopefully you will develop a habit for life and increasingly enjoy your walk with God.

QUESTIONS FOR REFLECTION

1. What is your biggest hurdle in trying to make time for daily personal devotion to God? How can you overcome it?

2. What are some ways that you can incorporate more praise and adoration into your quiet time?

3. Which acrostic—ACTS, CATS, TACS, or SCAT—do you prefer and why?

4. Why is meditation such an important aspect of one's devotional life? What is missing without meditation?

5. What do you think is the best way to keep one's devotional life vibrant, joyful, and alive?

ACTION POINTS

1. Because a habit usually takes at least three weeks to create, resolve to set aside at least ten minutes per day for a time of personal devotions, basic prayer, Bible reading, and brief meditation. Choose your place, time, and how you will approach the devotional plan. Try to have personal devotions in this manner for three weeks.

2. Set aside thirty minutes (the Lord's Day would be a perfect time) and, with a Bible or New Testament in hand, find a secluded area (a park, a field, a path in the woods, etc.) and take a "devotional walk." Pray, stop and read a Scripture passage (maybe a psalm), and then meditate on what you read.

PRAYER

"O Lord, as I enter into your presence, I confess that I give far more thought to life in the world and to my daily responsibilities than to life with you. Please grant me the resolve to set aside my cares and concerns, place them in your hands, and pause and spend time seeking you. May I find great comfort and assurance sitting at the foot of your throne and may I focus on things that are eternal while I live in the temporal. Meet me in the prayer closet, O Lord! I pray this prayer in the matchless name of Christ, who intercedes for me. Amen."[5]

5. The following is a list of some of the best books on the subject of prayer that I have seen or read:

Arthur Bennett, *The Valley of Vision: A Collection of Puritan Prayers and Devotions.*

E. M. Bounds, *The Complete Works of E. M. Bounds on Prayer : Experience the Wonders of God through Prayer.*

Ole Hallesby, *Prayer.*

Timothy Keller, *Prayer: Experiencing Awe and Intimacy with God.*

Douglas Kelly, *If God Already Knows, Why Pray?*

Paul E. Miller, *A Praying Life: Connecting with God in a Distracting World.*

George Mueller, *Answers to Prayer: From George Mueller's Narratives.*

Andrew Murray, *With Christ in the School of Prayer.*

Richard Pratt, *Pray with Your Eyes Open.*

Charles Spurgeon, *Spurgeon on Prayer and Spiritual Warfare.*

Appendix

The Three Domains Seen in
All of Life

This appendix is designed to demonstrate how the three domains of the heart are exhibited throughout so many aspects
of life in this world. I will belabor this point considerably so that
we might see the import of understanding the relationship the
three domains have with each other. Listed below are various are-
nas of life that we can explore as we observe the balance of the
three domains in our world.

THE THREE DOMAINS AND TEACHING

First, there is what educators call the three teaching domains. As
simple and as common as these are, they carry import in the classroom, in lesson planning, and in teaching (and preaching, I might
add). These three categories are:

1. Think (or Know)

2. Feel

3. Do

These educational domains can be expressed similarly:

1. Mind
2. Emotion
3. Will

1. Cognition
2. Affection/Inspiration
3. Volition

1. Knowledge (information and content)
2. Synthesis (understand the concept)
3. Application (to real life situations)

1. Thoughts
2. Attitude/Enthusiasm/Zeal
3. Behavior/Practice

1. Understanding/Belief
2. Acceptance
3. Commitment

1. Theorize
2. Internalize
3. Externalize

1. Indoctrination
2. Motivation/Intention
3. Action

1. Comprehension
2. Desire

3. Ability

1. Personal Knowledge

2. Personal Devotion

3. Personal Action

THE THREE DOMAINS IN LIFE

1. Learn

2. Love

3. Live

THE THREE DOMAINS IN THE CHRISTIAN LIFE

1. Upward—Knowing God (Head)

2. Inward—Experiencing God (Heart)

3. Outward—Serving God and others (Hands)

1. Logos—Knowing the Word (Truth)

2. Pathos—Passion for God and others (Love)

3. Ethos—Ethical appeal for living rightly/obediently (Righteousness)

1. Learning about God

2. Communing with God

3. Serving God

THE THREE DOMAINS AND THEOLOGICAL CATEGORIES

1. Systematic Theology
2. Spiritual Theology
3. Practical Theology

THE THREE DOMAINS AND THE HEART OF CHRIST

In the very stirring text of Matthew 9:35–38, when Jesus calls his inner circle of disciples to participate in his ongoing ministry, we read these words,

> And Jesus went throughout all the cities and villages, teaching in their synagogues and proclaiming the gospel of the kingdom and healing every disease and every affliction. When he saw the crowds, he had compassion for them, because they were harassed and helpless, like sheep without a shepherd. Then he said to his disciples, "The harvest is plentiful, but the laborers are few; therefore pray earnestly to the Lord of the harvest to send out laborers into his harvest."

Here, we clearly see the three domains in the heart of Jesus.

1. "*Seeing* the multitudes . . ."—Knowledge/Observation: Jesus is always watching, learning about, and understanding the needs of people, especially those who are spiritually searching and lost. His is a teaching and shepherding ministry and he is particularly attuned to those who are struggling, hurting, and disenfranchised by the established religion of his day. He *knows* the longings of the multitudes and the urgency of the task of helping them.

2. ". . . Jesus *felt compassion* . . ."—Deep Feeling/Love: The Greek word used in this text is transliterated as *splagchnon*. It speaks of the bowels or the intestines, but indicates deep-seated feeling and emotion. The bowels (or inner being) were regarded

as the seat of the passions. The Hebrews viewed the *splagch-non* as the place of deep affections, or as we would say today, "the heart." *Splagchnon* is the place of love. The emphasis is upon the fact that Jesus *physically* feels the spiritual needs of the multitude in such a way that his inner being is gripped and moved. The best analogy that I can use is what we call "experiencing butterflies" in one's stomach. It has happened to me twice, both times in baseball, while batting with the bases loaded in front of a large crowd of people. I was physically affected by the overwhelming circumstances. In our text, Jesus is physically affected by the overwhelming circumstances of people's spiritual needs.

3. ". . . therefore pray earnestly to the Lord of the harvest to send out laborers into his harvest." Work/Do: Jesus, having seen and being gripped with compassion for the multitude, turns to his disciples and charges them with engagement in the task of building his church. First, he translates the need he sees into the vision the disciples need to see: "The harvest is plentiful, but the laborers are few . . ." From the vision comes the call to prayer. All ministry must begin with prayer. From prayer comes involvement. The writer of this account, the disciple Matthew, tells us in the next chapter that Jesus chooses his inner twelve and lists these "laborers" by name. They will be doers!

THE THREE DOMAINS AND PRAYER

When we consider the subject of prayer, we recognize that the three domains must be placed in consideration in order for our prayers to be both biblical and acceptable before God. First, prayer must be based on Scripture, i.e., what do the Scriptures teach us about God as the recipient of our prayers? What do the Scriptures teach us about the nature of prayer (i.e., instruction regarding, admonitions about, and examples of prayer)? And, what do the Scriptures teach about the person praying?

The final question above leads us to the second domain, i.e., the nature of the feeling or emotive domain, or we might say "the attitude" of prayer. Prayer must be from the heart. Our motivations are significant to God. Humility, genuineness, and sincerity must punctuate the words with which we pray. Faith is essential (Heb 11:6). Willingness to hear God speak as well as submission to his will (again, Scriptures are priority) are also necessary attitudes.

Lastly, we must consider the third domain, that of action or doing. In prayer, the doing element is to be applied in the realm of discipline or work. Prayer is an endeavor. Although often spontaneous and practiced in momentary experiences of life, serious prayer usually requires designating a time for quiet and a place for solitude. It is here that the soul is able to pour itself out to the living God, who reveals himself as Father. The believer must set aside other distractions, which is a discipline in itself, and determine to spend structured and possibly lengthy time with the Lord. Such is the prayer that brings forth revival in the soul. Prayer is the effort to seek the Lord and is a means toward uniting the soul of the believer with his/her loving Father. Prayer can be very easy, like the flow of a longtime friendship, but it is also to be viewed as a discipline, a habit, and a deliberate effort. Prayer is not passive, except when the heart is stilled as it listens to the Holy Spirit speak through the active Word of God.

We might make the following conclusions about the integration of the three domains:

1. If prayer is based upon Scripture, but not from the heart, it becomes *legalism*.

2. If prayer is from the heart, but not based on Scripture, it has the potential to become a form of *false mysticism*.

3. If prayer is only used as a discipline or a self-justifying work, it becomes a drudgery without life or, for some, falls into an aspect of worship known as *formalism*.

THE THREE DOMAINS AND APOLOGETICS (DEFENDING THE FAITH)

1. Knowledge and Argument—includes presuppositional, classical, evidential, and rational apologetics. These approaches use knowledge, logic, and reason as a basis for defending the Christian faith.

2. Community—includes a reliance upon personal relationships, body life, unconditional love, and koinonia (fellowship) to convince others about the reality of Christian faith.

3. Life—includes setting an example, modeling, demonstrating integrity, and serving others as a convincing apologetic for becoming a Christian.

THE THREE DOMAINS AND THE NATURE OF CHRISTIAN CONVERSION

Dr. Will Metzger, in his classic book on evangelism, *Tell the Truth*, expounds on how the entire gospel needs to be explained to the entire person. The gospel appeal should include all three domains of the listener—thinking, feeling, and acting—and for true conversion to take place, the person hearing the message should respond to the gospel with the mind, the emotions, and the will. He goes so far as to state that the two elements involved in a conversion, both repentance and faith, should be experiences of the mind, the emotions, and the will. Although this approach appears a bit overly analytical, I believe that Dr. Metzger provides some legitimate insights into the nature of true conversion, as opposed to the many false or "easy" conversions that permeate present-day evangelicalism.

THE THREE DOMAINS AND CHILD RAISING

1. Know/Truth Domain: Catechize/instruct the child in the knowledge of the Lord and the Scriptures.

2. Feel/Love Domain (affection and respect): Express love for the child while teaching both a proper fear (awe and reverence) of the Lord and respect for the parents.

3. Do/Righteousness Domain: Demonstrate and require obedience, discipline, and the externals of behavior.

THE THREE DOMAINS AND WORSHIP

1. Cognitive/Creedal—often known as contemplative (thoughtful/reflective) in nature.

2. Emotive/Expressive/Inspiring—often known as celebrative in nature.

3. Behavior/Application—often seen as practical in preaching and response.

I should note that a God-centered and vibrant worship service should be comprised of all three elements. Some contemplative worshippers celebrate very quietly, however!

THE THREE DOMAINS FROM THE PERSPECTIVE OF MINISTRY

Luke 10:25–37: The Parable of the Good Samaritan, who crossed paths with a man who fell among robbers and was badly beaten. In contrast to the priest and the Levite, he . . .

1. "*saw him* . . ."—knowledge/observation of the man's plight or trial.

2. "he had compassion . . . "—expressed deep feeling for the man.

3. "*went* to him and *bound up* his wounds"—work/action on behalf of the needy man.

THE THREE DOMAINS AND THE SLOGAN OF REFORMED THEOLOGICAL SEMINARY

Another expression of the three domains is seen in the Reformed Theological Seminary motto (recently, but unofficially, perfected):

1. "A Mind for Truth . . .
2. A Heart (for God) . . .
3. A Life for Ministry"

THE THREE DOMAINS AND PREACHING/COMMUNICATION

1. Appeal to the mind
2. Elicit passionate engagement
3. Move/direct the will—application and behavior

THE THREE DOMAINS AND ART

John Ruskin, famous poet and art critic, once said that a good artist must possess three qualities:

1. An eye to see and appreciate the beauty of the scene he desires to catch on canvas
2. A heart to feel and register the beauty and atmosphere of the scene
3. A hand to perform—to transfer to canvas what the eye has seen and the heart felt.[1]

---

1. Cited in Sanders, *Spiritual Discipleship*, 102.

I would conclude by saying that as we expand our understanding of the three domains, recognizing that they are interrelated in every way, we can also better comprehend them as we analyze them separately. Separating them enables us to view ourselves and our proclivities, as well as understanding others and their inclinations. I am able to recognize much of this inclination toward one domain or another by observing various Christian denominations in our world today, as they emphasize different domains in their traditions. Some make education and theology a priority; others stress attitudes of love, mercy, and compassion; while others focus on hands-on mission and activity (sometimes known as "the social gospel"). The weakness of the "know" denominations is that they can become disengaged thinkers. The weakness of the "love" denominations is that they readily become doctrinally compromising. The weakness of the "do" denominations is that they substitute activity for doctrine and sometimes do so without love. Each tradition, however, can learn and benefit from the other, if it is willing.

Bibliography

Barna, George. *Growing True Disciples: New Strategies for Producing Genuine Followers of Christ*. Colorado Springs: Waterbrook, 2001.

Berkhof, Louis. *Systematic Theology*. Grand Rapids: Eerdmans, 1939, 1941.

Bennett, Arthur. *The Valley of Vision: A Collection of Puritan Prayers and Devotions*. Edinburgh: Banner of Truth Trust, 1975.

Bounds, Edward M. *The Complete Works of E. M. Bounds on Prayer: Experience the Wonders of God through Prayer*. Grand Rapids: Baker, 2004.

Hobbs, Becky. *How Big Is Your God?: The Spiritual Legacy of Sam Patterson, Evangelist*. French Camp, MS: RTSFCA, 2010.

Calvin, John. *Calvin's Commentaries*. Volume 7, *Isaiah 1–32*. Translated and edited by John King et al. Grand Rapids: Baker, 1981.

Demarest, Bruce, ed. *Four Views on Christian Spirituality*. Grand Rapids: Zondervan, 2012.

———. Lecture notes from RTS Charlotte course DM843, "Spiritual Formation & Soul Care for Ministry." July 9–13, 2007.

Hallesby, Ole. *Prayer*. Minneapolis: Augsburg, 1994.

Hull, Bill. *Choose the Life: Exploring a Faith That Embraces Discipleship*. Grand Rapids: Baker, 2004.

Keller, Timothy. *Prayer: Experiencing Awe and Intimacy with God*. New York: Penguin, 2014.

Kelly, Douglas F. *If God Already Knows, Why Pray?* Fearn: Christian Focus, 1995.

Lewis, C.S. *God in the Dock: Essays on Theology and Ethics*. Grand Rapids: Eerdmans, 1970.

Lloyd-Jones, David Martyn. *Revival*. Westchester, IL: Crossway, 1987.

Metzer, Will. *Tell the Truth: The Whole Gospel to the Whole Person by Whole People*. Downers Grove, IL: InterVarsity, 1981.

Miller, Paul E. *A Praying Life: Connecting with God in a Distracting World.* Colorado Springs: NavPress, 2009.

Mueller, George. *Answers to Prayer: From George Mueller's Narratives.* Compiled by A. E. C. Brooks. Chicago: Moody: 2007.

Murray, Andrew. *The Master's Indwelling.* Grand Rapids: Zondervan, 1953.

———. *With Christ in the School of Prayer.* New Kensington, PA: Whitaker, 2017.

Packer, J. I. *Keep in Step with the Spirit: Finding Fullness in Our Walk with God.* Grand Rapids: Baker, 2005.

———. *A Quest for Godliness: A Puritan Vision of the Christian Life.* Wheaton, IL: Crossway, 1990.

Phillips, Richard D. *Zechariah.* Reformed Expository Commentary. Phillipsburg, NJ: P & R, 2007.

Pollock, John. *A Foreign Devil in China: The Story of Dr. L. Nelson Bell, an American Surgeon in China.* Minneapolis: World Wide, for Billy Graham Evangelistic Association, 1971.

Pratt, Richard L. *Pray with Your Eyes Open.* Phillipsburg, NJ: Presbyterian and Reformed, 1987.

Ryle, J. C. *Holiness: Its Nature, Hindrances, Difficulties, and Roots.* Grand Rapids: Baker, 1979.

Sanders, J. Oswald. *Spiritual Discipleship.* Chicago: Moody, 1990, 1994.

Spurgeon, Charles H. *Spurgeon on Prayer and Spiritual Warfare.* New Kensington, PA: Whitaker, 1998.

Tozer, A. W. *The Pursuit of God.* Harrisburg, PA: Christian, 1948.